TARGET

THE WORK

THE WORKER

Effective **Employee Discipline** for Managers,
Supervisors, and Business Owners

Eric Lorenzen

Published by
Reader Hill
Yucaipa, California
readerhill.com

Reader Hill logo and colophon are trademarks of Reader Hill.

TABLE OF CONTENTS

Introduction

I have hired, trained, disciplined, and terminated hundreds of employees. Spend enough years managing in a high turnover industry and you will have a similar tale. Employees come and go. Some are great; some are stinkers. Most are good people who want to do a decent job. But even employees trying to do a good job will mess up and make mistakes. This book is about what to do when employees fall short of expected standards, whether they did so on purpose or unintentionally.

You and your business have standards that you require employees to meet. Those standards differ from business to business, but they usually cover areas like behavior, appearance, dress code, hygiene, attendance, attitude, work quality, work quantity, work pace, customer relations, truthfulness, following directions, and interactions with co-workers. Your business might be well organized, with those standards written up in an Employee Handbook, or your business might be more carefree with only have a handful of staff and standards that are informal rules like showing common sense, being a decent person, and working hard. But no matter where you fall on that spectrum, there are work standards at your business and it is part of your job to make sure the staff meets those standards. When those standards aren't met is when employee discipline is required.

Why do You Discipline an Employee?

That might seem like a silly question, but you should think it over. What is your motivation when you discipline an errant employee? Some see employee discipline as punishing a bad worker. Some managers look at discipline as a useless requirement that their own supervisors force them to do. Some use it as a chance to assert their power over others. Unfortunately, some managers can be skewed in their motivations. We should be disciplining an employee for their sake, because their behavior or work performance needs to improve. If you examine yourself and find that something else is motivating you, then work on getting that back into balance.

Even when we as managers have a healthier approach toward employee discipline, we usually hate disciplining others because we dislike confrontation. And yet discipline is necessary in any kind of endeavor. To accomplish something, whether that is building a rocket, selling cosmetics, remodeling a house, or providing office support, their needs to be an organized effort to be successful. There is structure, coordination, goals, and parameters. There are metrics and standards. This is work, not the frenetic chaos of a Kindergarten playground at recess time. An employee is hired to accomplish something, to perform certain tasks, to achieve particular goals. There is an *aim* to work, a target we are trying to hit.

As a manager or supervisor, your job is to help keep others aimed in the right direction, to make sure everyone is doing their part so that we can hit that target- that we can succeed. Now the definition of success changes by industry, company, and even department within a company, but we all have a success target in front of us. It could be a sales goal, customer satisfaction, accuracy in calculations, or the quality of widgets coming off an assembly line. You might even be supervising people who have different goals (like office staff and salespeople on a same team), but everyone has a job, a reason for being employed. Whatever the goals and metrics, it is your job as a boss to make sure that everyone on your team meets their goals and metrics. And one of your most important tools for reaching team success is *employee discipline.*

Employee discipline is when consequences are imposed on an employee for their failure to meet the standards set by the company. This is not something targeted at the person for *who they are-* that would be harassment or bigotry or discrimination. This is targeted at *the work-* because of something they *did* or *did not* do. A good boss knows the difference between the targeting the work and targeting the worker and makes sure to keep any discipline is aimed at correcting unacceptable behavior or performance.

So, why should we discipline an employee?

1. **Because we don't want to see a repeat of the problem.** This one's obvious. You discipline them because of something unacceptable that you don't want repeated. It might be something they did (or didn't do) or it might be for a bad attitude while on the job, but you can't have them doing it again.

2. **For the sake of the employee.** Truthfully, this is for their own good. You want every employee to be the best employee that they can be, and they can't do that if they don't know where they need to improve. The hope is that, through disciplining, you will get a better employee who does a better job.

3. **For the sake of the team and company.** By holding people accountable, you are helping the rest of the team. It can be demoralizing when they see others getting away with misdeeds or sloppy work or an unprofessional attitude. The rest of the team begins to wonder why they bother to do their part when someone's misbehavior is ignored or even celebrated. They start to see it as a double standard and they will start to grumble. If they are forced to cover another's slack, they might even grow resentful. So when you discipline you help to keep everyone else on track too. The rest of the team will be more motivated to work when they see you upholding the same standards on everyone. They might see you as tough, but they will also see you as fair.

What is effective employee discipline?

I wish that I could promise a discipline technique that was 100% guaranteed to reform any employee into a great worker. But I can't. There is no such secret method to motivate or prod an employee into maximum performance. However, this book isn't about being 100% successful; it's about being effective. Effective discipline involves three things: fairness, consistency, and appropriateness.

Fair. To be effective, employee discipline must be perceived as being fair. When employees think that a manager is letting someone get away with too much or someone else is being singled out for unreasonable discipline, then your employee discipline isn't effective. The same standards must be upheld with everyone- no favorites and no victims. While you cannot control what others think, you can do your best to discipline everyone the same way and to the same standards, instead of ignoring some or picking more on others. Be fair by keeping all employees to the same standards of professionalism and work performance.

Consistent. Effective employee discipline means that you don't change your expected standards from day-to-day. Your employees don't have to guess what the standards are today because they are the same as they were yesterday or a month ago. When employee discipline differs depending on a boss' mood or on whether a customer complained or not, then work suffers. It's hard to meet a standard that keeps shifting each day or even each hour. While the job might be dynamic with shifting goals and changing priorities (jobs in sales, consulting, and project management are examples), there should still be an expected standard of behavior and work performance no matter what else has moved.

Many companies create a written employee handbook specifically to provide that consistency. Both employee and manager can look it up in the manual and can see for themselves what the standard is for dress code or attendance or smoking on the job. Consistency is harder without a comprehensive employee handbook, but it isn't impossible. Just make sure everyone understands what the work expectations are and keep everyone to those standards every day. Be consistent.

Appropriate. The discipline should be appropriate for the severity of the offense. If you are seen as being either too lax or too harsh, then you can lose not only that employee's respect, but it could agitate the whole team. One of the reason I encourage managers to plan out a disciplinary meeting is to prevent hasty or heavy-handed discipline. Get your temper or fear under control, think through what you want to accomplish by disciplining this employee, and be purposeful in your disciplinary meeting. It is a matter of letting the "punishment" fit the "crime" and not seem either too light or too heavy. Not all offenses deserve a suspension without pay or a probation period. Some things need a verbal warning and that's it. Make sure your correction is appropriate to the problem you're addressing.

There is always the possibility that others will see your actions as wrong, but you can't control others' thoughts. Just do your best to make sure your actions are fit to the seriousness of the employee's misbehavior. The employee still might feel that you are *unfair* or *mean* or *wrong*, but most others will perceive it as appropriate and, hopefully, that disciplined employee will eventually come around to seeing that the consequences you imposed were appropriate.

The *honest communication of concerns* is necessary if we want a healthy work environment. Some will not want to hear the truth but we need to communicate it, along with imposing any necessary consequences. The better we are at communicating expectations to our team, the more likely they are to meet those expectations. Employees usually do better when they understand what is expected of them and know that they will face consequences should they fail to meet those fair expectations.

Improving at Employee Discipline

This guide book provides the tools for better employee discipline, so that you can be more consistent, more professional, and more effective. We will look at five areas:

- Basics of Discipline
- Your Employee
- Your Approach
- Your Meeting
- Your Follow-Up

The goal of the **How to Be a Better Boss** series is to equip managers, supervisors, and business owners with the knowledge and resources needed to be effective as a boss. In this book the aim is to improve your skills in employee discipline, because firm yet fair discipline helps create a stronger team and company.

So let's start by looking at the basics of discipline, including the four steps of progressive discipline and how to document a disciplinary meeting.

Basics

of

Discipline

Eric Lorenzen

CHAPTER ONE
Four Steps of
Discipline

"By the work one knows the workman."
- Jean de La Fontaine

The most common approach to employee discipline is called Progressive Discipline. The idea is to start with a verbal warning and, if that's not effective, to move on to a written warning, suspension, and then termination. The discipline gets progressively stronger when the employee is not showing satisfactory improvement. This does not mean that every disciplinary action must follow this course. More severe misdeeds may result in the employee being suspended or even terminated immediately.

Very often a company's employee handbook will have a section talking about their approach to discipline. Usually that section includes a paragraph like this one as a disclaimer to make sure that it's understood that not every disciplinary action has to first start with a verbal warning:

> The company has established a process of using progressive discipline that includes verbal warnings, written warnings, and suspension. This process is not formal and the company may use whatever form of discipline is deemed appropriate under the circumstances, up to and including termination of employment.

So Progressive Discipline is not meant to "tie your hands" as a manager, forcing you to take these 4 steps in order every time. Instead, Progressive Discipline is meant to provide consistency and fairness in any corrective action imposed. When employees feel that you are being fair- that your are holding everyone to the same standards- then they are more likely to work harder for you.

So let's take a little time to look at the 4 steps of employee discipline:

1. Verbal Warning

This is usually the first step in the discipline process. Use a verbal warning for minor offenses, but be sure the **employee understands it is a warning**. You need to be clear on this. The employee needs to realize that this is a warning and that you expect them to improve. This might be more informal and the employee doesn't have to read or sign anything, but this is still a warning.

This is not just an off-hand remark or a flippant comment about trying harder next time. Whenever possible, you should draw the employee aside and clearly indicate what the problem is, that this is a verbal warning, and explain how they should rectify the problem. For many employees, this will be enough of a warning and they will correct the problem.

Keep a record. A verbal counseling needs to be documented on a PIN (see Chapter Two, *PIN the Problem- Performance Improvement Notice*), but the employee does NOT see it nor sign it. Why make a written form about something done verbally? It provides a paper trail in case you have to take further action. It also helps when doing an employee's Yearly Review, so you can look back and see how long ago a problem happened or how often it occurred.

2. Written Warning

This step is usually used for repeat offenders or more serious offenses. The employee is expected to read and sign this form.

Employees need to understand the seriousness of the problem, so it is best to have an actual meeting to discuss the problem instead of just handing them a form to sign.

Sometimes you will have to write up an employee who is usually a good performer. To such a person a written warning may seem too harsh, so help them put it into perspective: typically, even good employees will accumulate a few written warnings over their years of employment.

Keep a record. This write-up should be placed in the employee's permanent file. You may want to provide them a copy if your Steps for Improvement section is rather detailed, but they don't receive the original PIN. Have them sign the original and then place it in their records.

Should each manager keep a copy of this write-up in their own files? Maybe, but only if kept in a secure place so that others cannot look at it; most companies will prefer to keep all such confidential personnel information in secure files in their office and not have extra copies floating about.

Adding a term of Probation: When dealing with a problem that will take the employee some time to correct, a probation period can help. Adding a Probation Period to a Written Warning creates an even stronger message to an employee who is failing to meet your expectations. Probation should be used sparingly, and should not be used in conjunction with just a verbal warning; the employee needs to see this in writing. Documenting that the employee has 30 days or 2 weeks or 90 days to improve sets a specific timeline for correction. This is more appropriate with issues of job performance, productivity levels, or correcting attendance problems.

When an employee refuses to sign a Written Warning: As seen in the sample PIN included in the next chapter, the sign-off section doesn't need to say that the employee agrees with the warning, only that it occurred and that they understand what it was about. If an employee refuses to sign even when it states that, then you've got a bigger problem on your hands. You've lost this person's trust and respect, and it's going to be even harder to supervise them. When this has happened to me, I'll push back by explaining again that their signature is not an acknowledgment of their wrongdoing- it is only an acknowledgment that the meeting has happened- and so there's no reason for them to refuse signing. If they still refused, then I knew that employee's time with the company would soon be over.

You have a few options when an employee refuses to sign even after being told that they are merely signing to acknowledge the meeting happened:

- **Option #1** is to let them refuse but make note of that on the form. Make sure the employee knows that you will make that notation in their permanent record and that you will still hold them to the improvement steps that the write-up tells them to do.

- **Option #2** is to add another write-up, this one for insubordination. Realize that doing this will probably anger the employee, but sometimes it's needed.

- **Option #3** is to escalate it even more to a suspension or even termination for that insubordination. Make sure you aren't doing this out of your own pride. The reason you might have to go "nuclear" over this is because the employee is completely unrepentant of their misdeeds and it is obvious they will now be impossible to supervise. Again, don't go this route out of anger or fear. Do option #3 only when the situation has completely collapsed and there is no way to redeem the employee. This might happen once or twice in your management career. If it happens often, then either you are hiring the wrong people or you aren't cut out to be a supervisor.

Even good employees can sometimes refuse to sign a write-up when they think it is somehow unfair or unjustified. Do your best to explain yourself, but realize that the two of you might never reach an agreement on what has gone wrong. They still might refuse to sign. So be it, but don't let the employee intimidate you. Don't let them think that they've gotten away without any consequences. They still need to be held to any Steps of Improvement mentioned in your write-up. Talk it over like two adults, make your final decision, and stick to it.

3. Suspension

This step is used only for rather serious or complex offenses. Often a suspension is time off *without pay* and should be for a set amount of time. It provides you a short window to investigate a complex problem (job injury due to a safety violation, a charge of discrimination, a fight at work, etc.). A suspension can also allow you the time to prep for a firing (final paycheck, list of company property to collect, locking the person out of the company computers, etc.)

Suspension while Investigating. This is done when something serious has happened but you don't have enough information to fire someone yet. It is a way to keep an employee away from work and/or co-workers. This is sometimes done when there are claims of harassment or discrimination as a way to protect the potential victims until you can discover the validity of the claims. This is also done when a serious accident or injury happens on-the-job, while you gather the needed details of what happened and who was responsible.

Suspension until Firing. If you or your employee are working at a remote location, you may have to suspend for one or two days (maybe *with pay*) while waiting for that final paycheck to be mailed to you from your corporate office. This is done because some states require an employer to pay a fired employee their final paycheck upon termination or within 24 hours of that termination. If that's the case, then you can't fire someone on-the-spot, no matter how grievous their misdeed. Instead, you send them home on a suspension until you can get the paperwork finalized. Be sure to check the applicable laws in your area to verify how quickly to get a final paycheck to a fired employee.

Note- usually, approved reimbursable expenses (like mileage or travel expenses) can be paid out later, once that now-fired employee gets the appropriate documentation submitted.

Keep a Record. I know I'm repeating myself, but it's so important that you do, especially when dealing with a suspension. The documentation should include the reason for the suspension, the dates of the suspension, and whether it is paid or unpaid.

Ending Suspension with a Time of Probation. There are times when you will bring an employee back from a suspension but put them on a probation to verify that they are improving. Set a time limit on that probation an make it clear how you are expecting the employee to improve during this time.

4. Termination

This is the final or ultimate step in employee discipline. You are firing this person because they haven't improved after numerous warning or because they've done something so egregious that they need to be let go. This is reserved for employees that 1) are already causing problems while still in their introductory period, 2) continue to repeat offenses that they have be written up for, 3) have too many write-ups for various topics, or 4) have committed a particularly bad offense such as job abandonment or theft. For more on the Termination Process, see Chapter Seventeen, *Termination Requirements*.

Keep a Record. You do not need to write up a PIN when firing someone, but you might want to make a record of the termination after it happens, writing down the details of when, why, how, and who were the witnesses. It could be helpful should the person make unjustified claims for unemployment benefits.

Which offenses call for a verbal warning and which a written?

I would discourage you from creating an official list of which offenses deserve to be written up. There are just too many variables to worry about. Instead, you may decide ahead of time the importance of compliance in various areas. Deal with general categories like attendance, safety violations, insubordination, dress code violations, poor work performance, leaving their work station messy, etc. For some companies, dress code violations are very serious because it hurts the company's public image or because a dress code violation is also a major safety violation in their field. That employee might not just get a written warning but maybe even a suspension. To other companies, a dress code violation is a mere verbal "please make a better choice tomorrow."

Decide, in general terms, how you want to handle each broad category but don't try to make a list of what is deserving of a verbal and what deserves a written warning. There are just too many possible variations and exceptions. In addition, you should consider each discipline problem individually, while still being fair and consistent with your whole team.

How many verbal warnings should you give before escalating it to a written warning?

Again, this is your own choice. Some offenses are not so serious or have extenuating circumstances, so you may give 2 or 3 verbal warnings. Other offenses may allow for only one verbal warning. Consider the number of verbal warnings and the time span between those warnings- three warnings in a week usually indicates a greater problem than three in a year. Overall, you want to be consistent and fair, disciplining all of your employees to the same standards and expectations.

Jumping Directly to Termination

The idea is that Progressive Discipline is your general approach to employee problems but is by no means mandatory. If I catch an employee stealing from the company, I'm not going to waste time doing two warnings before firing that person. Hopefully, that makes sense to you. Some misdeeds are so egregious that you should refuse to give the employee a chance to keep misbehaving.

Many years ago, when I was a district manager for a service company, I caught an employee faking her work hours. She claimed to be at a work location but wasn't there. At first I assumed that she had left for an early lunch, so I started doing some of the needed work myself while waiting for her to get back. But she never returned. Basically, she had come in that morning, documented her arrival, and then left for the day. She had falsified a full-day's work.

When I realized what she had done, I informed HR that she needed to be terminated and to get her final paycheck ready. They agreed and had it done by that evening. The next day I met her at that day's work location and I fired her. She made all sorts of excuses and pleaded for a second chance but I couldn't allow it. She had shown herself untrustworthy.

I have fired people for all kinds of egregious behavior, from working another job while on-the-clock to sexual harassment to job abandonment. Sometimes, an employee's misdeeds make it obvious that they aren't salvageable. This person needs to be removed and it becomes a question of how to do so quickly and legally. There is no need to go through a long process of verbal warning, written warning, and suspension. For some, you will need to go immediately to termination. (Again, see Chapter Seventeen, *Termination Requirements*, for more details on this process.)

CHAPTER TWO
PIN the Problem-
Performance Improvement Notices

Whenever an employee is disciplined for their work performance or on-the-job behavior, it should be documented. Some managers simply insert hand-written notes into an employee's file, but such impromptu notes don't always provide all the info that should be recorded. As a solution, I offer the simple idea of having a one-page form to document all of your disciplinary meetings. I've even included a sample version that you can either copy or modify for your own use. You can give your form its own name, but I'm calling it a Performance Improvement Notice (PIN), which is a common name used in the HR and management fields.

I think every manager should have this kind of form on-hand, ready to use as needed, because the form reminds you to record all the necessary info required whenever you discipline an employee. Keep the form simple- like I've done with the sample below- and succinct. Yes, there isn't much room to write your notes, but that helps you to focus on the main points.

Sample of a Performance Improvement Notice

Below is a blank sample of a PIN.

Performance Improvement Notice

Employee Name _____

Position _____ Date _____

Please Mark One:
- Record of Verbal Counseling # [   ]
- Written Warning Notice # [   ]
- Notice of Corrective Probation Period
  - From [   ] To [   ]
- Notice of Suspension
  - From [   ] To [   ]
- Record of Termination

Please Mark All That Apply
- Unsatisfactory Performance
- Unsatisfactory Work Quality
- Insubordination
- Failure to Follow Instructions
- Excessive Absences / Tardiness
- Rudeness / Unprofessional
- Damage to Materials / Equipment
- Violation of Company Policies
- Violation of Safety Rules
- Working on Personal Matters
- Misconduct
- Other _____

Reason for Performance Notice
_____
_____
_____

Specific Performance Problems
1 _____
2 _____
3 _____
4 _____
5 _____

Actions to Improve Performance
1 _____
2 _____
3 _____
4 _____
5 _____

Time to Improve _____

Next Disciplinary Step if Performance Does Not Improve _____

Supervisor / Manager

Name _____ Title _____

Signature _____ Date _____

Employee Acknowledgement (for Written Warnings and Suspensions only)
By signing this notice, I am acknowledging that I have been counseled and warned as noted above.

Signature _____ Date _____

PERFORMANCE IMPROVEMENT NOTICE   REVISED 8/2019

You can also download this sample at my website, EricLorenzen.com, under the tab "Forms": ericlorenzen.com/forms/

Why do a Performance Improvement Notice?

The aim is to 1) make sure an employee understands that their work performance or on-the-job behavior is not acceptable in a certain area, 2) show the employee what he or she must do to correct the problem, and 3) provide a written record of the disciplinary action that is consistent and easy to understand even years later.

What should be included in a PIN?

At minimum, a Performance Improvement Notice should include: 1) employee info (name, position), 2) date, 3) type of discipline (verbal, written, suspension, termination), 4) reason for the PIN and specific violations, 5) what is expected to improve that violation, 6) manager info (name, position, date, signature) and 7) a place for the employee to sign saying that they received this warning (if it's written or suspension). Let's look a bit more at why you should include these seven things:

1) **Employee info** is obvious, to make sure its placed in the right personnel file. Their position or job title is helpful if you need to refer back to this PIN years later for any reason, because employees do change titles/positions as the years go by.

2) **Date of the PIN** is vital (as is noting of the dates of employee misdeeds if this PIN covers multiple events) so that you can always be certain of when this problem happened. If the problem reoccurs then you won't have to try to remember how long it's been since you last talked to the employee. A quick glance at the employee's file will show the exact date of when you did the PIN.

3) **Type of Discipline** is again obvious. You need to make it clear to the employee and in your files what kind of discipline this is, whether verbal or written, and whether this includes a Probation or Suspension.

4) **Reason for PIN** and **Specific Violations** is where you first

summarize the problem and then list specific points about the performance problem or misdeed.

5) **Expected Actions to Improve** is the area where you explain what the employee needs to do to improve their behavior. This is what you will hold them accountable to do.

6) **Manager Info** and **Signature** is important, especially when you have more than one boss around. You can see who it was who did the PIN, which isn't always easy to remember when looking back at something months later. You can easily see who disciplined an employee and can talk with that manager if you need more clarification.

7) **Employee Signature** is not done for Verbal Warnings or Termination, but it is required for all other uses of this form. You'll notice that the sample copy has a particular phrasing to this section, saying that the employee has been "counseled and warned" as noted. By signing, they are not saying that they totally agree with the PIN, since most employees don't agree with everything their supervisor has said in a PIN. Their signature is just acknowledging that the meeting has indeed occurred and that they have been told everything that is written in the PIN.

What are the Legal Requirements when Disciplining an Employee?

At this moment, I know of no federal or state laws or regulations that mandate how or when an employer or manager can or cannot discipline an employee for their work performance or on-the-job behavior (within reasonable boundaries). Obviously, you cannot institute public flogging or anything else that is itself a violation of the law, but you certainly can discipline your employees and hold them accountable for their work performance and their behavior on the job.

Work Contracts and Union Agreements: If you have a formal contract with an employee or a union agreement that spells out discipline procedures, then obviously such a contract defines any limits or parameters set on employee discipline. You will need to work within the boundaries set by that agreement.

Contract Labor or Temp Labor: If you have non-employees working for you, then your ability to apply any discipline is obviously limited to the terms of the contract for those services. Be aware of the difference between actual employees and those who aren't. Non-employees include sub-contractors, service providers, personnel supplied by a temp agency, consultants, and anyone to whom your company is issuing a Form 1099 for tax purposes. You don't have the same authority over them as you would over an actual employee of your company. The parameters of your authority over their work performance should be spelled out in any contract you have with them or their employer. Those limits vary from almost-none over a repairman working on your copier to quite a bit of authority over a long-term human resources temp placed by an agency. Just because they aren't your employee doesn't mean they can do whatever they want, but it does mean your authority is limited to whatever the service contract states.

Avoid Discrimination. I will add this caution: you will want to avoid any appearance of showing favoritism among your employees, which can open you up to discrimination lawsuits. Numerous federal and state laws are in place to protect employees from discrimination due to age, disability, race, sex, religion, marital status, veteran status, and more. There are also laws against sexual harassment, bullying, and personal retaliation. So make sure that you are disciplining for a legitimate workplace performance issue, not because you're having a bad day or dislike someone.

You should be fine as long as your disciplinary action is handled professionally, both in its conduct/wording and by keeping it focused on work problems only.

Legal Requirements for Terminating: There are other laws to consider when firing an employee. Those specific regulations are discussed in Chapter Seventeen, *Termination Requirements*, so please review that chapter before firing or laying-off anybody.

Some cautions in wording of a PIN

A performance improvement notice can be subpoenaed for a court case, either concerning that employee or another employee's complaint. Done right, a good PIN will help your case. Done wrong, a PIN (or lack of one) can really hurt your company:

1. **Avoid references to personal life**- Leave out such references, unless absolutely necessary. Instead, keep it focused on the WORK problem and how you expect the person to correct their behavior or performance.

2. **Don't try to read their mind**- Using terms like "deliberately, willfully, maliciously, out-of-laziness, purposely" might make your warning sound stronger, but it could also look like a personal attack. Instead, focus on what the employee did, said, or failed to do. There is no need to try to predict their motives for messing up. (See Chapter Six, *You're Not a Mind Reader.*)

3. **Be specific about what needs to change**- Get to the point. What must change? By when does it need to change? What will happen if it does not change? Phrases like "do better", "don't let it happen again", or "stop doing this wrong" are not very helpful. Vague threats of "further action", "serious discipline", or "stronger consequences" are not very effective.

4. **Avoid legal terms unless really necessary**- Terms like "discrimination" and "harassment" are legal terms that can set off all kinds of alarms if they ever come up in court. If you really have either kind of problem, you will want to document and bring serious consequences on the offender. If the problem is less clear, then you still will want to document your discipline, but use language that is not so "legal". Consider phrases like "Your actions appear to violate the company's policy of showing respect to fellow workers" or "Your actions suggest that you may have created an offensive environment." You have to be firm and take action, but think about what you are writing. What if the offended person later sues for harassment or discrimination? Your PIN (or lack of one) might become part of the plaintiff's case. Watch out for extreme words, especially if you are

NOT taking extreme action.

5. **Be realistic**- When giving an employee a deadline by which to improve, some managers tend to write "immediately" every time. However, realize that some problems could take a little time to correct, such as work pace, attention to detail, error rate, etc. Set a doable deadline for their "time to improve".

How Long Should You Keep PINs in Personnel Files?

This is up to you, but many employers decide to make PINs part of an employee's "permanent record", never removing them. These records can help you when looking at any problems long-term, revealing any patterns over many months or years. The PINs can also help when doing a Yearly Review: has an employee improved (or worsened) over the whole year?

Eric Lorenzen

Your
Employee

Eric Lorenzen

CHAPTER THREE
Failing at the Task

"I tell you, sir, the only safeguard of order and discipline in the modern world is a standardized worker with interchangeable parts. That would solve the entire problem of management."
- Jean Giraudoux, French playwright and diplomat
The President in *The Madwoman of Chaillot* act 1

The French novelist and playwright quoted above was known for his ironic writings, but sadly many managers have wished for exactly what he described- employees who were like interchangeable automatons. In reality, each employee is different and unique. Any problems you will have with an employee will also be unique- different from the problem you had with another employee yesterday or the problems you'll face next week. Nonetheless, most employee issues seem to cluster into four groupings: communication, coordination of time, ability, and attitude.

Most often, when I have had to discipline an employee it was because they failed to get something done the way it needed to be done: be it a missed deadline, shoddy work, incomplete work, forgotten project, or just goofing off instead of working. Employee discipline was needed because of a problem with the performance of their duties. There were a few times when intervention was required due to personality conflicts or dress code violations or personal hygiene, but those were rare. Far more often, it has been a problem with failing at the task. The employee had a job to do and either didn't get it done or did it in a way that wasn't acceptable (too slow, too sloppy, incomplete, etc.).

I want to take a little time to look at why people often fail at a task, because when we understand the different reasons we can also see why different responses might be necessary.

4 Reasons for Failing at the Task

I've found it important to strive to understand why an employee failed to get a job done. Without trying to read their mind, I've come to realize that most failed tasks fall into four broad categories:

1. **Communication**- They did not understand what the task was or its importance to me.
2. **Coordination of Time**- They failed to complete the task in a timely manner.
3. **Ability**- They can't do the task.
4. **Attitude**- They won't do the task.

My response to the failure differs, depending on which category this particular failure falls under. With some of these categories, I might be partially to blame for the failure. Maybe I didn't communicate clearly. Maybe my time constraints weren't realistic. Maybe I never trained the employee on how to do this particular job. Maybe I've done something to offend the employee and so they no longer want to do their best for me.

So let's take a moment to look at these four reasons and how to handle them:

1. Clear Communication

In our rushed society, we as managers can fail to clearly explain what needs to get done. It will happen sometimes and it would be wrong to discipline employees when the fault lies more on us. Don't just assume they know what you want; tell them clearly. Some of the problem areas where communication can often break down is:

a) **New Tasks**: when this is something your employee has not done before you ought to take a more time to make sure the job is understood.

b) **Multi-Step Tasks**: when the job requires a series of actions that should be done in a particular order or at a certain pace, you need to confirm that the employee knows the order.

c) **If/Then Tasks**: if their particular tasks depend on something else (stock levels, customer response, etc.), make sure that they understand that fact.

d) **Cooperation with Others**: sometimes a task requires an employee to work with others, and that requires talking to others and working with them. When that breaks down, you'll need to ask who was at fault: yourself, the employee, or the other person(s) they were supposed to cooperate with.

e) **Failure to ask for Clarification**: the breakdown on communication can often happen on the employee's side. Whether due to shyness, pride, fear, or not caring, the employee doesn't ask you to explain something they were confused about. They just winged it. You can't read their mind to decipher why they didn't ask for clarification, but you can certainly hold them accountable to for not doing so.

Confusion is not an acceptable reason for failing at the task. Both the employee and the manager must take ownership of their part in causing the confusion. If the failure is due to lack of communication on *your part*, admit it and let them know you will do better next time. If the failure is due to a communication failure by *your employee*, then discipline accordingly. They also have a responsibility of asking for clarification if they don't understand.

2. Running Out of Time and Missing Deadlines

Some people are better at monitoring their time and keeping on track, but all of us need to hold to some kind of schedule. No employee should be allowed to ignore the time restraints of a job. Even a well-meaning employee can miss deadlines if they aren't working fast enough or letting themselves get distracted. How you will handle it is up to you. Is this the first time or is it a chronic problem? Was this caused by any extenuating circumstances like equipment failure or the employee being called away for another assignment? How important was the deadline that the employee missed? Did their time mismanagement cause problems for other employees or with clients?

The important question is how can you prevent it from happening again. Some possible solutions (in addition to any discipline) include:

a) **Model time management for the employee**. Take some time to work side-by-side with the employee, showing them how to keep on track.

b) **Assign a mentor**. Have a more experienced employee work with them for a few days to help them learn the best work rhythm.

c) **Set more intermediate deadlines** to make sure they are on track. Sometimes it can help adding in extra deadlines to help the employee set the right pace. (like "In two hours you should be done with step #4" or "By tomorrow you should have all the essential data on this spreadsheet and be ready to start creating the formulas")

d) **Set clear consequences** for missing another deadline. Sometimes you just need to be firm, making it clear that this cannot happen again. A new employee messing up is more understandable than a veteran employee who should know better.

3. When the Work is Beyond their Ability

There will be times when an employee just can't do the job you are asking them to do. Maybe they aren't strong enough. Maybe they don't have the needed education. Maybe it's beyond their cognitive acuity. Maybe it's outside their skill set. Whatever the reason, the employee doesn't have the ability to do the job required of them. (We're not talking about ADA accommodations for disabled or pregnant workers- that's a whole different can of worms; we're talking about a non-disabled employee unable to accomplish their job.)

Your immediate response to an employee unable to do a task will likely be a disciplinary meeting, but realize that isn't enough. You need to make a bigger decision here. If this particular task is beyond the employee's ability then it will never get done to a satisfactory level. If this is an essential part of that person's job, then the employee probably needs to be terminated. Other options are assigning that task to another, reassigning the employee to a different position, or arranging for assistance on this particular task. Arranging help is fairly simple if it concerns lifting a heavy supply box once a month, but accommodation is much harder when it's needed every day or maybe every hour. You will have to decide if it is practical to make changes on work assignments. The decision is yours, but make sure it is for the company's best and is fair to the whole team.

Just remember, inability is still not an acceptable excuse for failing at the task.

4. Refusing to do the Work

Sometimes you'll have an employee who just refuses to do their assigned task. They might make excuses or blame others, but when you get past those excuses they still will not do the work. They might claim it's not fair, that they are tired from what they've already done, or that this is not part of their job, but it's still refusing to do a task. This not an issue about ability; this is about attitude.

Convinced that They Know Better: You may encounter an employee who refuses to do what you've told them to do or refuses to do the work the *way* you've told them to because they think they know better. They might be a new hot-shot employee or they might be a grizzled veteran, but by doing it their own way, they're often causing problems elsewhere and they're certainly undermining your authority. You'll need to deal with their "failure to do the task" now, but you'll also need to decide what to do about their poor attitude toward you.

Is this an employee worth trying to keep? If so, then you'll need to figure out a way to work with them and (hopefully) earn their respect by your fair and strong leadership. Winning respect will differ with each employee. Some want to see you getting your *hands dirty* by working alongside them, while others want a boss who will *listen*. I've encountered some who need to know that their manager *knows more* than they do and others who need a boss who's confident enough to *admit their own mistakes*. The key to earning their confidence will differ by person so it can take a bit of time to figure out, but it's sometimes worth trying when an employee is worth trying to keep.

Blatant Rebellion: When an employee openly refuses your direction it's a direct challenge to your authority. Such outright refusal needs to be confronted quickly. If you try to ignore it, they will likely keep rebelling and might influence others to do the same. Be ready to terminate this employee rather quickly for their insubordination.

Refusing with Excuses: Sometimes an employee refuses to do an assigned task due to safety or ethical concerns. Such issues should be addressed appropriately. Legitimate safety issues need to be corrected; illegal actions need to be stopped. That's obvious. But the person complaining about safety or ethics might have a problem that isn't so black-and-white. What they see as unsafe, is fine if done carefully and according to established methods. What they consider unethical, might be legally permissible. Their problem is then a personal problem and not an actual matter of OSHA violations or law-breaking.

You will have to decide how to discipline this person for refusing to do a job because of their personal morals. Is this a one-time event or is this a problem with something that is an integral part of their work position or is it something in between those extremes? This could be a complicated decision and often depend on whether you want to keep this employee or not.

Sneaky Undermining: This type of work refusal can sometimes take longer to realize. Sometimes an employee's rebellion is done quietly, whether because they hate their job, just don't want to do the work, are envious of you, or are purposely sabotaging things. You may never know what their motivation was and it may take some time to notice the problem and trace it back to the culprit, but once you find out who did it you'll need to get rid of them. Whether they are doing this out of apathy towards the job or because of bitter hatred, it's doubtful that you'll able to reform this employee. Time for a quick termination.

Different Causes, Different Responses

So there are obviously many reasons why employees fail at a task, and because there can be so many different causes your disciplinary responses will also differ. This is where it can get tricky. You want to be fair, consistent, and appropriate in your discipline but you also will need to customize it to the employee and to the incident. In the next two chapters we will look a bit more at some of these complications and how to handle them fairly.

Eric Lorenzen

CHAPTER FOUR

Excuses and Explanations

"A bad excuse is better, they say, than no excuse at all."
- Stephen Gosson, *The Schools of Abuse*

"The dog ate my homework."

"But everybody else does it."

"What I did isn't as bad as _____."

"It's not fair!"

Welcome to the human race; we hate to be in the wrong. We make excuses for what we did (or didn't) do. We justify our actions. We provide explanations or point to extenuating circumstances. It's a common human trait because it's hard to admit when we've messed up. Don't expect different behavior from your employees when you confront them on their work performance or on-the-job behavior. Rare is the employee who will readily take ownership of their mistakes and errors. The better ones will accept discipline after getting a chance to tell their side of the story. The more immature ones might never admit to their shortcomings. But whether they took ownership or not, you will still need to discipline them. The work still needs to get done and they need to know the standard that they will be held to.

Listen to their Excuses (to a point)

During an employee disciplinary meeting, they will often provide excuses for what they did (or didn't) do. Usually, it's better to take their excuses at face-value unless you have good reason to know otherwise. Be willing to listen. Be willing to consider their side of the story. You might be surprised at what you learn.

Their excuse doesn't exempt them from discipline. I want to hear whatever an employee has to say, to hear their reason for why they didn't meet expectations. Even if I don't like what they say, I want to hear it because it reveals what that person is thinking or feeling. I might not agree with their excuses but it's good to know how they are justifying their actions. That does NOT mean that their excuse justifies their shortcoming.

Drop your need to have the employee agree with everything you say. Sometimes an employee will not agree with all of your claims. They may admit to parts of what you're disciplining them for, but still refuse to own all of it. That can be frustrating, but don't let that turn your disciplinary meeting into a heated debate. Be careful that you aren't digging in your heals, wanting them to admit to everything without any asterisks or exceptions. Surrender your need for total submission to your superiority. If your ego is that fragile, then get out of management and get yourself into professional counseling. This is not warfare; you are not trying to totally conquer and subjugate your employees. You are simply correcting an employee's job performance or work behavior, and making sure they understand the standards they will be held accountable to maintain.

Limit blame-shifting. Sometimes an employee tries to get out of trouble by pointing at others. Usually, I would listen to this up-to-a-point but then I would bring the conversation back to the employee and what he or she did. Even if others have misbehaved, it doesn't justify what this particular employee has done. I'll admit that there have been a few times when I've suspected the wrong person of a mess-up, and then I have corrected myself and made sure to discipline the correct person. However, I've found that most finger-pointing was done to try to justify their own misbehavior. I would still discipline the employee, but then I would consider whether I also needed to discipline the others mentioned.

Some Explanations will Change Your Mind

By allowing an employee to talk during a disciplinary meeting, you might just learn that you've made a mistake. The employee could give you an explanation that either proves that the misbehavior you suspected never occurred or that your interpretation of it is faulty.

Be willing to admit when you're wrong. Let an employee share their side of the story. Sometimes what they say isn't what you assumed about the situation. It can be eye opening when you realize you were seeing things wrong and that it looks very different from the employee's perspective.

Be careful that you don't resist legitimate explanations just because you want to win the argument and force them to see things as you do, for them to legitimize your own actions. Instead, be open to what they say and you just might learn that you've been wrong about this. You might be disciplining the wrong employee or you maybe you shouldn't be disciplining anyone at all.

Upholding Objective Standards

Rare is the manager who wants to be considered heartless, but sometimes our desire to be nice and compassionate comes in conflict with our responsibilities as the *enforcer of standards*. There is a job that needs to get done. If an employee can't get that job done, then something must be done to correct it.

There can be many reasons why an employee failed to get the job done (See Chapter Three- *Failing at the Task*), but if the work isn't up to standards, then something needs to change. You cannot expect everyone else to take up the slack or for customers to accept poor service; you certainly can't fill in and try to do the employee's work in addition to your own. This needs to be corrected and done so in a fair way.

Temporary Shortcomings. There will be times when an employee isn't working at their best due to circumstances: an injury, illness, personal loss, upcoming life event (like marriage, divorce, baby), and so on. That employee might have to take a break from working until their condition improves. Maybe you'll need to urge that employee to take a Sick Day, Grief Day, or short-term Leave of Absence. (Be aware that pregnancy is often treated as a temporary disability under the law and does require some accommodations.)

Sometimes you might have to order an employee to clock out immediately and go home, especially if they are a health risk to themselves, co-workers or to customers- you don't need someone coughing and sneezing on everyone. There are times when the best answer is for that employee to not work for a short time, for their own sake and for the sake of others. The time off might be with pay or without (depending on your company's policies). It should be for a short time. It might require a doctor's release before you will let them return. Temporary shortcomings like illness happen in the careers of every employee, so be ready for them. Know your company policies so that you handle each event fairly.

Other times you'll keep them on the job but you'll firmly remind them that the work still needs to get done. No one wants to be perceived as the wet blanket that's trying to dampen another's emotions, but you can't let one person become a major distraction or hindrance to the rest of the team. If all that they want to do is talk about the upcoming happy event or share memories of dearly departed grandma, you might have to intervene and insist that they limit their sharing for breaks and time away from work. If you ignore their disruptive behavior, you're allowing them to sabotage the performance of the whole team. Don't excuse that kind of behavior, even if it is done without ill intent.

Ongoing Shortcomings. There are other times when an employee isn't working well and there isn't much hope for a quick turnaround. It might be a lack of necessary education, physical weakness, ongoing depression, chronic illness, or addiction. Remember that you are their manager, not their doctor, personal trainer, professor, or counselor. You cannot fix them; that's not your job.

When you realize that you're dealing with an employee with an ongoing problem, you might need to plan on how to replace them. Sometimes you can shift responsibilities and make it work without burdening others on your team, but that can't always be done. Sometimes that employee's ongoing shortcomings can't be compensated for. When their issues can't be offset, then you'll have to deal with the fact that they are just too weak, too ignorant, too lethargic, too drugged, too…

You'll still need to go through the proper steps of discipline and give them a chance to improve their performance, but the odds are against them. They might surprise you and make huge improvements but it likely will not happen. Most likely, you will be firing this employee within a few weeks or months, depending on how grievous their shortcomings are.

This is hardest when you have an employee who means well but just can't meet expected standards. It can be heartbreaking to let such an employee go, but it still needs to happen. During my time as a retail manager, I had an employee who was a recovered addict. He really wanted to do a good job but his short-term memory was shot from his past drug abuse. You could remind him of tasks every hour and he would still forget. Among other things, he would leave the cash register unlocked and unguarded. When told of his error, he would apologize and try to improve, but he couldn't. It was beyond his abilities. In the end, I had to let him go. As much as I wanted him to succeed, his ongoing problems weren't something I could ignore. The work had to get done and he wasn't able to do it.

Ultimately, you as a manager have people that you report to (be that your own boss, the company owner, or your customers) and those others expect your team to get certain things accomplished. Don't forget that it is your job to lead the whole team, not just the one you feel sorry for.

Disabilities. Sometimes an employee might never be able to work up to expected standards due to a disability. The law offers certain protections for employees who are disabled and you should learn about those laws and how they apply at your workplace. When possible, you should try to develop an accommodation for that employee that doesn't put an undue burden on your other employees. Maybe they can excel at their job with some adjustments. Consider it before you fire them or drive them to quit.

The law doesn't make disabled employees untouchable, nor will you be forced to employ them no matter how awful their attitude or work performance. However, you might want to consult a competent lawyer on how best handle a problem employee who is disabled. You most certainly will want to document all steps you take to try to accommodate that employee's disability. Be fair but realistic. Sometimes, you will have to let go of a disabled person because they can't do the work even with realistic accommodations. Just follow the proper steps of employee discipline while also treating them with the dignity they deserve.

Standards Remain

No matter the excuse or explanation, the standards at your business remain the same. If something isn't up to that standard, then a change has to occur. While talking to an employee, you may get greater clarity about the problem but the problem is still there. You might learn that the solution you intended will need to be tweaked to work or that the problem-causer is someone other than who you suspected, but either way you will need to bring correction and make sure that the "something" is no longer beneath company expectations.

There will be times when the problems you encounter will have a deeper root cause and that can require a stronger response on your part. In the next chapter we'll consider the difference between issues caused by performance and those caused by character.

CHAPTER FIVE
Performance vs. Character

"Character is simply a habit long continued."
- Plutarch

Some employee shortcomings are endemic and will not be easily changed. These are problems deeply embedded into the person; it is almost a part of *who* there are. Call the issue a flaw, habit, personality quirk, or something else but it's impeding their work performance or hampering the team. These are character issues that are long-term and hard to escape.

Other employee shortcomings are more of a performance issue that can often be corrected when a manager calls out the problem and insists on change. These are things that can be fixed by better training, the right resources, or just an employee being aware of the problem and taking the effort to correct it.

You need to be aware that there are big differences between Performance Issues and Character Issues.

What is a Performance Issue?

These are short-term problems that can be fairly easy for an employee to correct. It might require learning a new skill, concentrating better, changing a behavior, or not taking shortcuts. Usually a warning will cause the employee to improve, or at least try to improve. A performance issue is not a habit that an employee must break.

I once had an employee who was a hard and honest worker but who had a body odor problem. He worked so hard that he would sweat and get stinky, which was not appreciated by customers. It was awkward to pull him aside and talk about a need for deodorant or cologne, but I did. It was embarrassing for him to hear, but he listened. He fixed the problem and remained a great worker. Issue resolved.

Dealing with an employee's performance issue. Problems with employee performance are much easier to deal with than character issues but that doesn't mean that the discipline path is the same every time (see Chapter Three, *Failing at the Task*). To explain what I mean, let's look at some common performance issues and possible causes. Only when you can answer "Yes" to the three questions will it be time for disciplinary action. If you answered "no", then you probably need to correct the problem on your side before demanding better performance from your employee.

1) **Work Pace.** When an employee is working slower than expected, you'll need to consider possible reasons why.
   a) Is the expected pace realistic? Yes or No
      (Consider the speed of comparable workers)
   b) Does the employee have all the tools and resources necessary to work at the expected pace? Yes or No
      (Hard to keep up when you don't have the right equipment, software, or information)
   c) Was the employee properly trained at that task, what steps to follow, and what priorities to set? Yes or No
      (Make sure they know how to do the job correctly before you insist on speed.)

2) **Work Quality.** When an employee's work is not meeting expected quality levels, you'll need to consider these possible reasons:
   a) Are your quality standards realistic? Yes or No
      (Could most employees reach the expectations you've set, or is only attainable after decades of experience?)
   b) Has the employee been trained on how to reach the expected

standards? Yes or No

> (Expecting a certain level of quality without showing how to attain that level is a cruel way to manage.)

c) Does the employee have the time and resources needed to maintain the standards expected? Yes or No

> (Hard to keep up standards when being constantly rushed or under-supplied.)

3) **Behavior at Work**. When an employee is acting unprofessional on the job, you'll need to consider these possible reasons:

a) Is this behavior being done intentionally? Yes or No

> (Sometimes an employee is not even aware of their misdeed, policy violation, or rudeness)

b) Are others held to the same standard? Yes or No

> (Make sure you aren't ignoring company veterans or friends who are also misbehaving and getting away with it)

c) Do you have all the relevant facts in this situation? Yes or No

> (There might be another side to the story. Someone else may have provoked the employee's bad behavior.)

So if you were able to answer "yes" to the questions, then you're ready to discipline that employee. If you answered "no" to 1 or more of the questions, then you have some work to do to correct things. Even if you are still disciplining, you will probably leave out those issues that your employee couldn't control.

There are still things for you to consider and investigate, but overall a performance issue is rather straightforward. Giving an employee a verbal or written warning doesn't guarantee that they will improve but, when the problem is due to a performance issue, there is a greater chance that the employee will correct the issue and you will get a better employee out of it.

What is a Character Issue?

Sometimes an employee's problem has a bigger cause than just their performance. Sometimes the problem comes from something that is deeply ingrained in that employee. These types of problems are very hard to change because they involve the employee's nature. Things like dishonesty, addictions, personality quirks, repetitive misdeeds, and laziness are in this category. An employee may want to change, but it will not be an easy process because it usually involves a habit formed over many years.

A person who is regularly grumpy and grumbling will not turn into a perky, everything-is-sunny employee just because you had a talk with them. They might learn to be more polite to others and professional in their behavior but it's doubtful that this person will become the team's new bubbly cheerleader. Be real in your expectations.

An employee who likes to brag and exaggerate will not easily become a humble and unassuming person just because you warned them to stop being so obnoxious. They might get better at controlling their tongue in certain settings (like bragging about the past sales numbers at company meetings) but don't expect a total transformation. You might be able to get them to correct their habit in a limited scope or in a particular setting, but they will still be a braggart everywhere else. That's just facing reality.

That employee who is late to work, late to meetings, and late for almost all other deadlines is usually dealing with a character issue too. Whether they are a bad time manager, live a harried life, or come from a family heritage where time is inconsequential, this is an issue that is set deeply into their life. Unfortunately, for most jobs an employee who cannot keep on schedule is a liability.

Dealing with an Employee's Character Issue. You will need to decide if this character issue is small enough to keep working on or if it is too big a problem: like the difference between someone who has a habit of exaggerating (but still works hard) and someone who regularly lies about what they did that day. Sometimes character issues can be fairly easy for you and your team to adapt to, like a personality quirk or shyness or grumpiness. You might say that we all have character issues in us, be it bad habits, emotionally sensitive areas, or our personality. As long as those character issues are relatively benign in the workplace- the issues don't really affect our work performance- it shouldn't really be an issue at all.

Sometimes you may have to make an adjustment to an employee's responsibilities to better play to their strengths (like moving the person who hates confrontation away from the store's customer returns counter). The issue can be turned into a non-issue be simply recognizing it and giving that employee a better defined role or specific coping tools.

I once worked with someone who had no sense of empathy toward others. He was blind to other people's feelings and views. However, he was a good worker when he worked on his own and received quite a bit of praise for his job performance, so upper management thought he would be a good manager. They were wrong, of course, because they hadn't taken the time to learn about this guy's character issues. Within months, his entire team rebelled and told upper management that they would all quit unless he was removed. The guy was that terrible at understanding the people on his team- their needs and motivations. You might say he was tone-deaf to other humans. Upper management had to face their mistake; he was an awful choice for supervisor. To their credit, they demoted him back to a regular worker and he grudgingly went back to his former job still not understanding how he had messed up as a manager. He was just clueless to his own lack of social skills. He did well back at his old job, though he was now a bit grumpier and just a tad resentful. His character issue could be worked around when he had no one under him. He could work well with *things* and *processes* but not with people.

Character Issues can be Job Killers. Not at all character issues are benign. Not all issues can be worked around. Some problems can be lethal to an employee's performance or to their ability to work with their team. Issues like a rage habit or paranoia or laziness can destroy not only that employee's job performance but also sabotage the output of the rest of the team. It's hard to work with someone you fear or distrust. The problem might be bullying, lying, constant unwanted flirting, repetitive tardiness, or any number of other issues.

The character issue becomes a job killer when it makes that employee toxic for the company. When that happens, you're only option is to get rid of the employee. Don't delay, because then more damage could happen to your team, your company, and your own reputation as a manager. You need to be firm and pro-active on this. Follow your company's discipline steps (typically verbal warning, written warning, suspension, and then termination), giving the employee a fair chance to reform, but realize it will most likely not happen. It is even harder when the employee is nice and well-meaning but their character issue can't be corrected or worked around, and it's that character issue that makes them an anchor that will just sink everything else. No need to give them extra time to correct the problem, just give them a fair opportunity like you would anyone else. They might surprise you and get their issue under control and finally meet company standards, but that rarely happens.

Don't drag your feet because you feel sorry for the person or because you fear them or because you're too busy right now or because you hate having to find a replacement. Get it done. This is one of those hard decisions that all managers have to deal with.

In the next section, we will look at your approach to disciplining employees. We will consider some of the common errors that can hurt your effectiveness.

Your Approach

Eric Lorenzen

CHAPTER SIX
You're Not a
Mind Reader

"Men see a little, presume a great deal, and so jump to the conclusion."
- John Locke

Have you ever noticed a stranger who looks in normal health and yet they have parked in a handicap spot? I have and I'll admit that sometimes I've wondered if that person might be "borrowing" someone else's handicap placard to take advantage of a privilege they have no right to use. And that might be true. But it also might be true that this person has a handicap that isn't so obvious to the eye. I can't easily tell if their heart is sound or their lungs are good. I don't have any idea of their medical history or current condition. I can't tell what's going on inside. That's why I try to not judge anyone using a handicap spot that has the appropriate tag. Instead, I try to be thankful that I don't need to use a handicap parking spot myself.

In a similar way, we cannot tell what's going on inside our employees. We don't know their thoughts, emotions, history, personal struggles, distractions, hang-ups, dreams, or fears. We have no idea what might have been their motivation. Sometimes an employee doesn't even know themselves why they did what they did. Trying to read their mind or guessing at their motivations is a fool's quest. You're more likely to guess wrong and offend them with your assumptions and accusations. Better to keep the conversation on the facts before you: something was done wrong at work and it needs to be corrected.

Examples from Failed Mind Reading

There are many managers out there who really think they can read an employee's mind, and most likely you are one of them. At least, you've been guilty of trying. I've been guilty of it too. Now you probably don't call it mind reading, but whenever we jump to conclusions or guess at the motivations behind another's actions we are guilty. We are trying to read their mind.

"I know what she really thinks about _____"

"I bet he got dumped by another girlfriend. Look at how distracted he is."

"Obviously, her home life is interfering with her work."

"You said this, but I know you really meant _____."

This is not a helpful game to start playing. In truth, I really don't want to know what stuff is racing through someone else's mind; I have enough of a challenge trying to figure out my own thoughts.

Quest for the Why

The empathetic manager may be tempted to try to understand *what an employee might have been thinking* when they did what they did. Don't go there. Mind reading is NOT your superpower, so stop trying to do it. I'm not saying that you should suddenly turn into a heartless ogre, but you need to keep it focused on **what** was done instead of trying to guess **why** it was done.

The employee might provide the *why* during your disciplinary meeting, but that is up to them to explain and not for you to guess at or for you to demand that they share (at least not if this has something to do with their life outside of work). Realize that usually you don't need to know why they did what they did. Learning the *why* can be helpful in understanding extenuating circumstances or motivations, but it isn't necessary.

Stop prying into their personal life. You need to realize that many employees do not want to share their feelings or the reason behind what they did. Something very personal might be happening in their life that is none of your business. They might be dealing with pain, loss, or confusion. As long as the employee takes ownership of their workplace mistake and shows a willingness to change, then you shouldn't pry. Control your desire to fix the employee's problems that aren't work related.

Often, our life outside of work influences our work performance. When a sick kid keeps you up all night, you'll be tired at work the next day. When a car has to go into the shop, it can be hard to get to work on time. When stressed about finances or big life decisions, it can be hard to concentrate at work. However, many employees don't want to share about their personal life, especially when they are having difficulties. They certainly don't want to talk about it with their boss. Do your best to respect that desire to keep their personal life private. Your concern isn't their life outside of the workplace, it's their performance while on the job. Curb your curiosity and respect their privacy.

Your objective is not discovering the *why*. Remember this, the objective is not for you to understand why your employee did wrong. The objective is to make sure the employee understands what they did wrong and that you expect them to now correct it. It's not about you. It's not about your employee's feelings. It's about correcting a problem and getting back on course. When a manager is questing for the *why*, they are getting away from the actual problem.

Often you don't need to learn more about this problem; it's the employee who needs to learn, to understand. You are having this disciplinary meeting to make sure the employee knows that their actions were unacceptable and must improve. This is not a therapy session nor is it an inquisition.

Your Assumptions Can Make it Worse

Guessing at the reasons *why* an employee did something could lead you into bigger trouble. Your guess might sound like an accusation.

Your guess might even lead to a lawsuit for harassment. Just because another employee messed up because of _____, doesn't mean that's the same motivation for this employee. Just because this employee once had a problem at home that hurt their work performance, doesn't mean that is what happened this time too. Just because *you* once had a problem with _____, doesn't mean *your employee* has the same problem. Projecting feelings and motivations onto an employee is a dangerous game.

Stop assuming you understand their motivations. You can waste hours trying to guess why someone acted as they did, and your final guess can often be wrong. You might think they purposely sabotaged someone else's work, but in reality they were just being absent-minded... or it could be the reverse. Too much of this guessing game and you could turn into a paranoid boss who thinks everyone is out to get you. Therein lays madness for a manager.

As I said earlier, sometimes an employee doesn't even know themselves why they did what they did.

Keep your focus on the problem instead of the motives

When disciplining an employee, keep the conversation focused on the work issue. You don't want to detour into what might have motivated their misbehavior. Even if they want to volunteer to share their personal problems, don't let this turn into a pseudo therapy session. Bring the conversation back to the work problem at-hand. It isn't your job to solve their issues that aren't work related; you're not their parent or counselor.

As a manager, you need to remember to do your job too. If you let an employee distract you with issues that aren't work related, you may end up failing at your own duties. Showing some sympathy is fine but you still have your responsibilities, so work hard to control any disciplinary meeting. Don't let the meeting get hijacked by other topics. You can show compassion for an employee's life problems while still holding them to same standards everyone else in the company is required to meet.

Eric Lorenzen

CHAPTER SEVEN
No Excuses
from You

"We keep the faults of others before our eyes; our own behind our backs."
- Seneca

"Are you going to let him get away with this?" I asked the manager I was training.

We were standing in an aisle of a retail store (the company we worked for provided services for that big-box chain). I was talking about the employee who had just blatantly disrespected this manager. The employee had gone out to his vehicle to retrieve some supplies for the project we were working on, but he hadn't returned. Instead, the young man spotted a good-looking customer and had asked her if she needed help. He then spent the next 10-15 minutes escorting her around the store helping her complete her shopping list. His flirting was so obvious that he got congratulatory high-fives from store workers as he finally wandered back to us, smiling with pride at what he had just done.

His manager offered a weak excuse about it being hard to hire in the area.

"You have to confront his behavior," I pressed. "If he acts like this when you're here, what is he doing when you're not at the store?"

I wish I could say that the manager shaped-up and firmly called out his employee's wrongdoing. But it didn't happen that way. Instead, the employee got a watered-down, weak talking-to. The employee replied with claims that he was just providing customer service (even though our customer was the store, not the individual shoppers). The manager's attempt at discipline crumbled and he tried to "move on" to the project that had been interrupted by all these antics. The employee also willingly "moved on," knowing that he had gotten away with his little stunt.

Neither that district manager nor the employee lasted long, for both were failing at their jobs. The employee's misdeeds were obvious, but the manager's failure was even worse. By failing to confront a performance problem, he was creating an anything-goes atmosphere. By not confronting the misbehavior, he was saying it was okay to act that way. By accepting such behavior a manager is introducing a poison that can sicken a whole organization. If not stopped, it will cause even good employees to start slacking off and cutting corners, for they will grow frustrated when they see a co-worker obviously misbehaving and getting away with it.

Don't miss that: allowing misbehavior can poison your whole team.

No More Excuses

We like to be liked, so very few of us enjoy confronting another person. Frankly, a boss who *does enjoy* confronting others probably shouldn't be in any position of authority. But enforcing standards, rules, and minimum performance expectations is an integral part of any supervisory position. If we can't hold workers to those standards, then we shouldn't be their supervisor, because then we aren't doing our job.

You were picked to be their leader, whether you are the one who hired them or not, and sometimes that means you have to bring correction to those employees. No employee is perfect. No employee does their job flawlessly. They need a leader to help them stay on-track in their work performance, even though you as a manager aren't perfect either.

Feeling like a Hypocrite. Sometimes a manager can be hesitant to discipline an employee because he or she knows that this is a weakness for them too. How can you demand something that you can't live up to yourself? That's a legitimate question and sometimes it's a wake-up call to your own mistakes (like tardiness or slow pace or bad attitude), but you have to remember that your employee's performance is being held up to an objective standard (company rules, performance goals, etc.) and not as a subjective comparison to your performance. You are not disciplining them to "act more like me." Instead, you are disciplining them to "meet the expectations of the job."

Although it is good for a manager to set-the-example by working as hard and as competently as everyone he or she supervises, the truth is you will always have employees who are better than you at some things. Frankly, you may be overseeing people who do work that is beyond your skill level. They know more, work faster, or generate more sales than you ever could. The more specialized or diverse your team is, the more likely this is to happen. You may have specialists who have degrees in areas that you've never studied. You might have experts on staff who have worked in their particular field longer than you've lived. Admit that to yourself but don't let that intimidate you from disciplining them. Again, the standards are not your own work performance or skill level; the standards are the objective standards of the job. Whether they are generating more sales than you ever could is unimportant. Are they generating the amount of sales expected of all salespeople? Whether you understand the intricacies of what they are assembling is not as important as whether they are assembling that product at the speed and quality level required.

You need to get the focus off yourself and get it on the expected standard for the job. If the employee isn't performing to that standard, then you discipline them, always pointing to that objective standard. It's not about you and your shortcomings; it's about that employee doing the job they were hired to do and doing that job to expected criteria.

Fear of Confrontation. Learn to be comfortable in confrontation, because every disciplinary meeting is a confrontation. You are meeting to point out a problem and to make sure the employee understands what they must do to get it right. Sometimes the confrontation will be minimal and the employee will quickly admit their error and promise to correct it. But those are rare. Often, the employee will disagree with you or make excuses and then you will have to push the issue, leading them to admit their error and agree to what needs to change. (See Chapter Fourteen, *What: Control the Conversation* and Chapter Fifteen, *Show the Way* for more on how to guide an employee to facing their errors and finding a way to improve.)

If you hate confrontation, then either step down from management or learn techniques to cope with your own issue. This might mean rehearsing your meeting beforehand or even writing out notes or a script. You aren't the only manager whose heart starts pounding and palms get sweaty at the thought of confronting another person. It isn't easy to do, but you need to push yourself to get more comfortable with this vital part of your own job. It doesn't mean that this will ever be fun or easy, but you need to be competent at discipline.

Worried about Consequences. Sometimes a manager avoids disciplining an employee because of what might happen. *He won't like me anymore. She'll get angry. He'll quit. She'll get upset and tell others on the team. He might get violent.* The excuses are nearly infinite and those fears can seriously hamper your ability to do your own job. Out of fear of the employee's reaction, you let their misbehavior or poor performance go unaddressed and likely it will just get worse.

That doesn't mean ignore the real possibilities of a bad reaction, especially if you fear for your safety. It might mean that you need to be more purposeful and plan for that confrontation, but it will still need to happen. Worried about an angry reaction? Maybe you need to confront that employee in a more open setting, still offer some privacy but hold the meeting where others can notice if something goes wrong. Try the warehouse floor away from others instead of in an isolated office. Maybe you need to have another person present at the confrontation (preferably another manager), so that they can be a witness to whatever is said or done.

If your fear is that the employee will suddenly quit and leave you in a lurch, then maybe you need to start looking for a replacement even as your prepare for your disciplinary meeting. There are times when you might need to soften your discipline to avoid immediate consequences, but do that only if you have a greater plan. That greater plan might be going easy on this mediocre employee until a replacement employee is ready. That greater plan might be getting company policies in writing within the next month so that there can't be any more excuses of not knowing the policies. That greater plan might be shifting employee responsibilities or reassigning personnel or doing more cross-training so that no employee is completely indispensable. The offending employee still needs to know that you aren't accepting their poor performance or bad attitude, but you are softening the blow so that they stay around long enough for you to get in a better situation. I think this approach should be used sparingly, but I have done it a few times for the good of the company.

All employee discipline has consequences, but not always bad consequences. The hoped-for consequence is that the employee will now do better. Even if the employee gets upset, throws his work apron at you and quits, it might still bring about good consequences. The rest of the team might be encouraged by the removal of a bad apple. The rest of the team might gain more respect for you.

Curse of the Best Buddy

Beware of this trap. Managers can fail at their job by becoming too close to some of the people they supervise. Others on the team might think you give special treatment to your friends (whether you do so or not) and that can sour the others and ruin team performance. The workplace turns into two groups: insiders and outsiders. Insiders might feel they can get away with more misbehavior because you're a friend. Outsiders might grow resentful of perceived slights, favoritism, and lost opportunities to advance. Your friendships could ruin your effectiveness as a boss.

Friendship is a top motivator for most employees. Just because you are now a supervisor doesn't mean that the desire for friendship disappears. You will still appreciate workplace relationships. Obviously, the best place for you to develop friends would be among your fellow managers or with people outside of work, but that doesn't always happen. The reality is that you spend more time with your employees than you do with almost anyone else outside your immediate family. You get to know them, you go through deadlines, project challenges, mistakes, and fun times together. Sometimes, a friendship develops and soon you are having lunch together, sharing personal stories, and enjoying each other's company. Then it moves on to other after-work activities, like barbecues, parties, movies, or concerts. Some managers and employees can handle keeping work and friendship separate, but many cannot. For them, the line between work and friendship blurs.

Excusing the misdeeds of friends. Your employees who are also friends may have a hard time seeing you as "boss" when at work. They might be shocked if suddenly their "friend" gets tough with them about meeting a deadline or tells them to start working harder. Even good employees can be tempted to take advantage of a supervisor who is also a friend. *I'm late but John will understand; he was with me last night at the concert.*

That buddy mentality will also make it harder for you to discipline that friend. Now you are not only getting an employee upset; you are risking the end of a friendship. Giving in will be a huge temptation, but if you ignore the shortcomings of your buddy you'll likely alienate the rest of your team.

Workplace Romance. Some friendships go even further; they spark a romantic interest. If you are tempted that way, you must resist or one of you must go work elsewhere- either to a different section or with a different company. It is a huge no-no to be romantically involved with anyone who reports to you. Most companies forbid such behavior because it opens the door to sexual harassment lawsuits if/when the romance turns sour. Even if that romance stays strong, it will aggravate the rest of the team because they know that their co-worker is getting special treatment from their supervisor. Just don't mix romance and supervising.

Avoid the Curse. Keep away from the Curse of the Best Buddy by keeping a professional distance between yourself and those you supervise. Be friendly but not friends. This is especially hard if you have been recently promoted from among your former peers. If needed, make a plan to develop new friends either among your fellow managers or with people who don't work there. It might be hard at first, but it will help you in the long run.

Eric Lorenzen

CHAPTER EIGHT
Watch Your Attitude and Style

"Condemn the fault, and not the actor of it."
- William Shakespeare, *Measure for Measure*

When we provide correction to an employee, we can either *help* or *hinder* our work by how we present ourselves. Our stance, eye contact, tone, and general body language is either supporting or contradicting what we are trying to say. In all of it, remember that you aren't here to condemn your employee, but rather to "condemn the fault" as Shakespeare said above; you are simply and truthfully declaring an action as wrong. This isn't about humiliating the employee but about getting a problem corrected, so you want to approach it with the right attitude. If you take the time to prevent any misunderstanding, you'll have a much better chance to see improvement in your employee.

Don't Let Your Anger Have Control

When disciplining an employee, it's best not to aggravate,

intimidate, or come across threatening, and that can happen if your anger is out of control. Uncontrolled anger on your part will often bring an extreme response from an employee. They might fight back- with words or fists. They might run- quitting on the spot. They might get revenge- getting you fired or suing you. Most certainly, the employee will lose any respect they had for you if are abusive toward them.

Anger needs to be controlled. Quite often when you are confronting a problem, you will be upset. Someone did something wrong and now you're angry. You're mad at what happened. You're mad at having to take the time to do this. You're mad at this person. However, that anger needs to be controlled if you want to be effective in bringing change. Don't let that anger run free or you will likely say or do things that will get you into trouble. Cussing, throwing objects, hitting things, or even threatening the employee can result when your anger is uncontrolled.

You may be justified to be angry, but get it under control before you try to discipline. Obviously, sometimes you need to stop something dangerous immediately- *Stop swinging off that ladder! Take that contaminated food off the grill!* -but most of the time you can take a pause between the violation and your rebuking of it. If needed, take a walk around the building or go get a drink of water. Get that anger under control before you try correcting the problem.

You don't have to be perfectly calm when disciplining an employee, but you do need to be emotionally controlled. They should know you're upset about what they did, but they should also know that this is about that particular wrong and not about them personally.

Don't try to dominate or subdue into silence. It's the insecure manager who needs to shout or lecture, demanding that the employee listen without a word. You are not trying to subdue an enemy nor are you trying to force them to yield to your greater wisdom. Work on being secure enough in your position to let them talk and even disagree with you.

Never make personal threats. Sometimes it's appropriate to threaten someone's job, telling them that if they don't shape up they'll get fired. However, it's never okay to threaten them personally. Uncontrolled anger often causes verbal attacks on the employee rather than attacks on the misdeed. Anger can make it personal and then you attack the person instead of what the person did.

Sarcasm and Jokes Aren't Appreciated Either

Your tone of voice can really affect whether a disciplinary meeting will work or not. Misplaced humor can sour a meeting as badly as uncontrolled anger. Even chit-chat and light-hearted jokes can seem wrong to people during a disciplinary meeting because this is a serious moment to them.

Sarcasm and Belittling is wrong. If you are prone to being sarcastic or snide, you need to control it during any disciplinary action. Too many people have had rotten parents, coaches, or teachers who belittled them as kids, telling them they would never amount to anything. You might think you are being funny, but not everyone will take it that way. For many, those words will rip the scab off an old wound and they will react badly.

Your little side-remark might blow up into a fight, just because you couldn't control your tongue. Instead, keep it professional and avoid the snide humor.

Joking and Banter usually aren't appropriate either. Being too light-hearted can be offensive to an employee too. No one likes to be disciplined at work, and usually that warning is placed into an employee's personnel file. To most employees this is a serious matter and they expect you to treat it as such. Joking or being too flippant might just imply that you really don't care what happens to them. Now is not the time to try to build camaraderie or to be a buddy to them. Instead, keep it to the subject at hand (the problem you're confronting) and keep it serious.

The banter about sports or weather or the latest movie can wait for another time. Respect your employee by taking this disciplinary interview seriously. Keep on task and get to the point. This is not the time for small talk. Instead, address the problem and how it can be corrected.

Watch Your Non-Verbals

People can say a lot without ever opening their mouth. Your body stance, eye contact, and hand motions speak things about you. This can help or hinder an employee correction. You need to be careful that you don't alienate or confuse an employee with your non-verbals. You also don't want to falsely judge an employee by their non-verbals.

Cultural Differences: One important fact to remember is that we are a diverse society. Various cultures express feelings differently. Even within the same culture, one family can have different non-verbals from another. Here are a few of those differences:

1) Your **proximity** to another: in one culture it might be rude to get closer than 6 feet to another person, while in another there is no problem standing nose-to-nose. Respect your employee's distance boundaries; there is no reason to make this disciplinary interview uncomfortable by invading the personal comfort zone.

2) Making **eye contact**: some cultures consider eye contact to be essential, while others consider it to be rude when done towards an older person or a superior. Don't judge their reaction to your disciplinary interview simply because of the eye contact or lack thereof.

3) Making **hand gestures**: some cultures or families are just far more expressive with gestures to emphasize a point, while others see such movements as rude or even threatening. For some, a pointed index finger is a huge insult. Try not to offend or intimidate the employee with your hand gestures.

4) Making **physical contact**: some cultures or families enjoy shaking hands, hugging, or touching a shoulder. It is a way to show companionship and to emphasize a point. If you are that way, please restrain yourself during the disciplinary meeting, or you might face a harassment suit or an assault claim. One person's friendly touch might be seen by another as belittling, flirting, sexual

harassment, or even as a physical attack. During a disciplinary interview the physical contact should be limited to a handshake at most.

Confusing to others: Remember that it is not always easy to understand non-verbal signals (See Chapter Six, *You're Not a Mind Reader*), so don't try to map out all of your employee's personality traits and quirks. How you perceive someone's body language might not really reflect their views or feelings, so try not to judge your employee's reactions based solely on their non-verbals. (If they say they heard you, don't question it just because they didn't make eye contact.) Instead, try to be more sympathetic toward their cultural idiosyncrasies, to realize their non-verbals actions don't always mean what you think it means.

More important than your employee's body language is your own. You want to effectively discipline them; you want to see their performance improve. To do that, you want to make sure that your body language isn't confusing or upsetting your employee. You don't have to become paranoid about your "signals" but maybe you can correct some things that are easily misunderstood. It's worth a try.

Mixed Messages, also known as the Sandwich Approach

Another failure to communicate when disciplining can happen when you try to sugar-coat your words. If you cover things with too much sweetness an employee might end up leaving your disciplinary interview thinking it was a commendation. Not only will the problem not get corrected, the employee might think you want them to do that misdeed more often. Talk about confusion.

Imagine a schoolboy who decides a particular girl would be the perfect girlfriend for him. He pursues her with all he has and really becomes a pest, and she's getting tired of it. She wants to let him know that she's not interested but doesn't want to hurt his feelings, so she tries the sandwich approach. She starts with a compliment. Something like, "*You're a really nice-looking guy.*" That's the bread on the bottom; the start of the sandwich. Then she moves into the meat of her conversation. Something like, "*I just don't want to be in any relationship right now. I'm focusing on school and sports.*" The middle of this sandwich is often kind of skimpy. She moves quickly to top the sandwich with another praise. Something like, "*Almost any girl would be happy to date you, but I'm focused on school right now.*" Afterward, she might be convinced that she handled that well, telling him she's not interested and doing it in a nice way. Unfortunately, he might have missed the center of that sandwich and noticed only the compliments she started and ended with. He might even double his efforts of pursuing her, because she thinks he's cute and now just needs to be convinced that it is the right time to start dating him.

Many employee disciplinary meetings have gone as awry as that girl's attempt to correct the boy's behavior. Hemming and hawing around the topic just causes confusion. Compliments muddle the message. In an attempt to be nice, the manager has failed to really discipline. It's just a big mess of mixed praise and complaints that leaves the employee uncertain of what went wrong and if they are expected to change something.

Avoid the Sandwich Approach and leave most of the compliments for another time. Instead, be concise in your disciplinary meeting, explaining what the problem is and what you expect the employee to do to fix it.

The nicest thing you can do is be straightforward about the problem and clear about your expectations on how they should improve in that area.

CHAPTER NINE
Use Group Rebukes Sparingly

"Discretion of speech is more than eloquence."
- Francis Bacon, *Essays: Of Discourse*

I hate group rebukes. I hated them in school, when a teacher was trying to pressure the class to snitch on a troublemaker or when a coach was trying to shame the laggards who didn't do something up to his expectations. And I really hated group rebukes at work, when a boss would chew out the whole team even though only a few in the group were the offenders, because I usually assumed that I wasn't one of them.

Doing a group rebuke is like using a sledgehammer to trim a bush: you might get that errant branch shortened but in the meanwhile the whole bush gets mangled. A sledgehammer is a great tool, but you need to use it for the right kind of job. Most often, a smaller tool, like pruning shears will do a more precise job. Similarly, a disciplinary meeting with just one or two employees can often be much more effective than rebuking everyone in a public pronouncement. A group-wide rebuke might seem more *efficient*- you only have to talk once- but it isn't necessarily the most *effective*.

What is a Group Rebuke?

This happens when you call together a group of employees and proceed to vent your frustrations at the whole group, even though the problem was only caused by some or maybe just one of them. You're not calling out anyone in particular for a public shaming. Instead, you are splattering everyone with the debris from your wild sledgehammer swing. A group rebuke is the opposite of a company pep rally- it's gathering everyone together for a chew-out session.

Why do managers rebuke everyone? Reasons can vary. Some do it because they hate confronting someone face-to-face, so they would rather give a vague message to everyone in hopes that the right person gets it. Some do it out of laziness, not wanting to bother finding out who the real perpetrator is. Some do it in hopes that the team will then discipline the wrongdoer. Some fear the violator so they'd rather act like everyone has messed up.

Other times, a manager can do group rebukes because they like to. It can feel good as a boss to let out your feelings in front of everyone. It can feel empowering to scare the whole group with warnings or threats. If you are someone who likes to rebuke everyone at one time, you need to ask why you are doing this. Is it really necessary? This shouldn't be just so you can vent and let off some of your anger and frustration; you're trying to lead these people and get the most out of them.

Sometimes a Group Rebuke is Justified

Even though I personally dislike group rebukes, I realize that there are certain times when it will be the right approach to discipline. For this to be a successful group chew-out, you'll probably have to do almost all of the talking and do your best to avoid calling out individuals for rebuke (not wanting to humiliate or shame anyone). You'll also want to keep tight control of such a meeting to prevent it from turning into a blame session where people start pointing fingers at each other. The idea is to present the problem and then propose your solution to it. You might solicit comments from your team about additional ways to solve things (but keep it away from accusations against others). You might ask them to come and talk to you individually if they want to share their ideas. But if this turns into a blame session you'll have an even greater problem on your hands, like shattered confidence, distrust, hurt feelings, and anger.

So let's look it three possible reasons to have a group rebuke:

Group Failure. Maybe the whole team missed an important deadline, performance goal, or expected quality level and that failure was brought on by many (if not all) of the group. If it is something the whole team is held accountable for, like a collaborative project, then they need to learn to do their part to police the actions of others in the group. You will most likely have to own up to your part in the failure too, since you are their leader.

You'll often see group rebukes in sports because it does take the whole team working together to win the game. And sometimes this will apply to work as well, when everyone needs to work together to complete a project by the deadline or to reach a company sales goal or to make a detailed presentation to a client. Know your work setting. Some jobs demand a lot of collaboration while others are much more individualistic. If your team demands people working together to complete the work (think of all the subcontractors and specialists that go into manufacturing a warship or a space rocket), then a group rebuke might be necessary if there is a major failure in the group's performance. But even in a highly collaborative setting, you should try to nip the problem early, before it requires gathering everyone for a rebuke.

Major Change in Your Approach. Another reason for a group rebuke is a way to signal to the whole team that you are becoming more serious about everyone's performance. If you've developed a reputation as being too nice and easygoing about company standards, then sometimes a very public change of attitude is needed. It is a way of declaring that- from now on- everyone will be held to a higher standard. Such a group rebuke is more about the future than it is about what has already happened. It's a warning to everyone that you'll no longer tolerate mediocrity or rule-breaking or a slow work pace. You can't hold this type of group chew-out often, but there are times when it is needed because you've let things slip for too long and everyone now needs to know that the "new me" won't tolerate it anymore.

Major Change in the Business. A group rebuke might also be appropriate when the company is being forced to make a major change, because it's something that will affect all employees. Maybe mediocre performance was acceptable due to lack of competition, but now everyone has to maintain a far higher standard to reverse a steep decline in sales. Maybe the previous owner allowed a lot of freedom with compliance to company policies, but the new owner is expecting everyone to adhere to the established procedures. Maybe a major new client is expecting a much higher level of work quality and performance. Whatever the reason, when there is a major shift for a whole team, division, or company, then all the employees should be informed and doing so in one large meeting is an efficient way to tell them.

Will your group rebuke produce the results you want? It might if it is for one of the reasons mentioned above, but more often it will be ignored by the very people who really need to shape up.

Reaching the Wrong Employees

Too often, a group rebuke is ignored by the very problem employees that you were trying to warn. Maybe they don't care. Maybe they think you don't know that they were the ones that messed up and now think they can keep on goofing off. Maybe they're clueless and don't realize you're talking about them. Whatever the reason, the very employees who need to hear this don't listen. They may have felt the whoosh of air as the sledgehammer rushed past them but they are clueless of their close-call with getting smashed.

So who did feel the brunt of your hammer swing? Most likely, it was your good employees. The very ones who didn't need to hear the rebuke. They heard it and now they are angry, upset, feeling unappreciated, stressed, or worse.

-You rebuke the whole team for poor performance and now the hard workers think you are setting an impossible target specifically for them.

-You rebuke the group for tardiness and long breaks and now the good workers think you don't notice when they show up early and instead are keeping tabs on every second they are late to their work station.

-You chew out the team for failing to meet a monthly sales goal, blaming their laziness for that miss, and the great workers lose much of their motivation to keep selling since you think they are lazy anyways.

-You vent about uncaring employees and a lack of work ethic, and now the good employees think you don't even notice all that they are doing to help the company succeed. Why bother putting in the extra effort when nothing gets noticed?

Hopefully, you can see why a Group Rebuke can often cause more problems than it solves. Those who pay attention to a group rebuke are often the very employees who don't need to hear it, while the trouble-makers and layabouts ignore the rebuke completely.

Vague Words and Generalities

Another reason some managers use group rebukes is to avoid obvious confrontations. This type of meeting is only half-hearted in rebuking and turns into more of an urging for everyone to try harder. Sometimes the manager won't even own their part in upholding company standards, but will talk about the need to please those higher-ups like the company owner or the corporate office. "*Look guys, we gotta get this done because the big shots are insisting on it. I know it's not fair, but we need to try.*" This manager is acting like they're just another worker, taking no responsibility for supporting company standards. They are also undermining their own authority.

Weak group rebukes also spare the manager from having to confront anyone one-on-one. To this manager, a disciplinary meeting might seem too antagonistic, too argumentative, too mean. They think it's better to issue vague warnings and requests to "do better" to the whole team than it is to deal with individuals.

Choose a Disciplinary Meeting Instead

Most often, it is more beneficial to hold individual meetings instead of doing a group rebuke. It will take more effort, because you'll need to find the real culprits instead of blaming everyone. It will take more time, because you will have to hold multiple meetings if you have more than one problem employee to address. And yet, meeting one-on-one is often more effective, because the employee will have no doubt who you think is to blame. Instead of being vague, you are being specific about the *who*, which is a big step in the right direction. You've identified who is responsible for the problem.

In the next section, we will look at what goes into an effective disciplinary meeting. We'll consider where to hold a meeting, how to prepare for it, and the direction the conversation should take.

CHAPTER TEN
Be Firm
and Fair

"She openeth her mouth with wisdom;
and in her tongue is the law of kindness."
- Proverbs 31:26 KJV

Employees mess up, and when they mess up it needs to be confronted or it will keep happening. I think that's common sense to most of us, but how do you confront the problem so that it isn't repeated? Well, the most important point to effective employee discipline is NOT attacking the employee personally. I'm not talking about taking a swing at them (though you shouldn't do that either), but I'm talking about verbal attacks. Words like:

"How stupid are you?"

"Fool! Stop that!"

"Are you purposely trying to mess up?"

"Are you trying to bankrupt me?"

"Anyone with a half a brain knows better."

I could have mentioned another hundred phrases that are personal attacks. Use them and you're not berating what was done, you're attacking the person who did it. Say these kinds of things and you're failing as a manager. You don't deserve a pat on the back. Instead, you're asking for a punch in the mouth.

A good manager will distinguish between the problem and the

person who caused the problem. A good manager is careful in their aim and proceeds into employee discipline with firmness and also fairness.

You can be kind in your words while still upholding company standards. There is no need for personal attacks. You show wisdom when you hold firm to expected standards and treat everyone fairly.

Target the Work, Not the Worker

I just want to re-emphasize the title of this book. It's not just a catchy phrase. Effective employee discipline is targeted at the work and not the worker. You need to make it clear that your problem is not with the employee as a person- your problem is with the behavior. They did (or didn't do) something. Keep your focus on the *action* and not the *person*.

Intimidating or mocking employees isn't effective long-term. Calling them names or making fun of what they did is an abuse of your authority as a manager. Unfortunately, some of us had that kind of behavior modeled to us as the way to lay-down-the-law. Maybe you had a bad parent, teacher, coach, or previous boss who got their way by embarrassing you, but I doubt you liked it when they did it. Why repeat that abuse on your own employees?

Please realize that you are shaming and humiliating a person when you verbally attack them. It might work short-term, intimidating that employee into behaving, but it usually fails eventually. Any employee with a healthy self-respect will not put up with such abuse for long. They will either fight back or flee and most likely they will not stop resisting you until either they or you are gone.

Publicly humiliating anyone is cruel. Sometimes, a manager will rebuke a person or a group of people in front of others. The manager might "call them out" in front of co-workers, in front customers, or even in front of their family or friends. By doing so, that manager is publicly shaming and humiliating them. As the actor Rip Torn said in the quote above, you shouldn't do that to anyone. Your victim(s) won't be motivated to do better; they will more likely be motivated to revenge.

Frankly, when you publicly humiliate an employee, you'll likely demoralize everyone else; they will fear similar treatment should they ever slip up. So, while it may have felt good to embarrass that problem employee, it likely caused more problems for you. Resist the temptation to shame anyone. Instead, take that individual aside and deal with them only. And keep the conversation on the problem, not the person.

Be Careful in Your Targeting

When targeting an employee's work, make sure your message is clear and to-the-point:

Target your PIN tightly. It is best to write a Performance Improvement Notice ahead of time, making sure to state the facts clearly- keep it rifled in on the issue you're addressing. Don't do the shotgun approach which scatters shot over a wide expanse of problems and issues, for that will often fail to bring change. Spreading your PIN to *cover everything* a little bit will usually confuse rather than inform. When an employee gets a PIN that covers too many different topics, they'll often have trouble realizing what's most important to you. If needed, do two PINs at the same time. It's not ideal to do that, but sometimes a whole cluster of problems happen at the same time and by separating the PINs you can properly emphasize the two issues that are your top concerns.

Target your words accurately. What exactly is the problem? Make sure you explain it clearly in a way that your employee will understand. Some managers start a weird type of management babble when in a disciplinary meeting, trying to use terms they learned in college or in a seminar. Using academic slang or acronyms that your employee doesn't know is unhelpful, so avoid the professional insider language. Instead, try to keep it simple and ask questions during the meeting to make sure they understand what you've been sharing. Make sure your disciplinary meeting doesn't fail because you failed to use the right words. You want them to understand. You want the employee to grasp what the problem is and what they need to do to improve, so don't try to impress with fancy words or vague references or inferred threats. Instead, talk normally and plainly.

Aim for your intended results. Always keep in mind what you want to accomplish when disciplining an employee. Is this about fine-tuning the performance of a decent employee? Is it about throwing down the gauntlet- *either shape up or get out*- with a lousy employee? You'll discipline differently, depending on the bigger results you want to see happen- the first might be done in a gentler tone while the second might call for a blunt PIN with strong consequences listed if they failed to change their ways. Will you accomplish your intended results? Not always, but you'll be more likely to succeed if you purposefully aim for it.

Be Firm in Discipline

A firm manager is someone who means what they say, someone who doesn't just make idle threats or empty promises. To be firm in discipline means that you will consistently hold your employees to the expected standards. Being consistent means that you avoid extreme swings in your discipline. You'll be the same whether you're happy or grumpy that day, whether sick or healthy. Being consistent means you don't let up on the essentials, but keep everyone to the same high standards. Be known as a manager who keeps to your promises and warnings, following through just as you said you would.

Be firm not soft. Being soft and gooey might be great traits for caramel but not for managers. Sometimes, when a manager hungers for approval by their employees, the manager becomes too permissive and lets problems go unaddressed in the hopes that the employees will appreciate them for their kindness. Often that doesn't work. Instead of liking you more, the employees will instead just lose their respect for you. Many misbehaving employees won't see your leniency as an act of kindness; most won't even notice it. The ones who will notice are the good performers and they will become resentful. In you attempt to be nice to the problem employees, you'll alienate the good employees and they will lose their desire to work hard. For the sake of your whole team, don't go soft on employee discipline.

Be firm not brittle. Being consistent doesn't mean you can't be a manager willing to change things when it's appropriate. You don't want to be so set-in-your-ways that you turn brittle. A good manager is willing to bend and change when situations change over time.

Sometimes, the rules or standards can get off-kilter as work conditions alter. You don't want to be so hardened in your ways that you can't acknowledge that circumstances have changed and now something may no longer be as important as before (or something that was previously trivial is becoming vital). Such changes happen over time with work processes, dress codes, company procedures, client relations, and more. If you have the ability to make policy changes, do so. If someone else has that power (your supervisor, corporate office, the company's owner), then bring the need for change to their attention. Don't just ignore things when a standard has become imbalanced, but you still need to enforce the standards as fairly as you can until they are reset. Fight for any needed change, for your own sake and for your employees' sake. After all, company standards should make sense to you and to your employees.

Be Fair in Discipline

As I said at the beginning of this book, employee discipline must be perceived as being fair. When employees think that a manager is letting someone get away with too much or someone else is being singled out for unreasonable discipline, then your employee discipline isn't effective. The same standards must be upheld with everyone- no favorites and no victims. You will be far more respected for being fair than for being nice.

Here are ten things you can do to help show your fairness in discipline:

1. Treat every employee with respect
2. Hold every employee to the same standards (no favorites and no victims)
3. Prove the violation by pointing to written policy (if no written policy then remind them of verbal instructions or appeal to

common sense)

4. Show them the consequences of their actions (how their violation causes problems for them, for others, and for the business)
5. Take the time to listen to their side of the story
6. Be willing to admit whenever you're wrong or have a part in the problem
7. Accept that employees will disagree with you (and yet you still need to uphold the standards set)
8. Work hard to keep your anger or frustration aimed at the problem and not the person
9. Offer a clear instructions on how they can do better
10. Don't hold grudges (once this is settled, don't keep holding it over their head for weeks or months)

Simply put, fairness is how you would want to be treated. Treat your employees like you want to be treated and you'll go a long way in becoming a fairer boss.

Bringing it All to the Meeting

We've talked about the basics of discipline, about your employee, and about your approach, but now it's time that we started talking about your actual meeting. In the next section we'll talk about the *when*, *where*, *how*, and *what* of disciplinary meetings as well as the importance of *showing* your employee the path to improvement.

Your
Meeting

Eric Lorenzen

CHAPTER ELEVEN

When: Control the Timing

"Delay is the best remedy for anger."
- Seneca, *De Ira*

Sometimes you have no choice- you must discipline immediately. Sometimes you need to stop someone in the midst of doing something stupid, illegal, or even deadly. There's no time to pull the perpetrator to the side and explain what's wrong; you just yell out "stop!" However, most actions deserving of discipline aren't a go-directly-to-jail kind of offense. For most problems, you can pick the time to discipline. You might delay just a few minutes (enough time to calm down so that you don't scream at them). You might need to delay for a week as you investigate a more complex violation, like a claim of discrimination. Either way, you should be in control of the timing. The disciplinary meeting happens when you are ready, not when the violating employee feels they have the free time.

Give Yourself Time

Delaying a disciplinary meeting for a little bit is often best, if it gives you the time to do the following:

Time to collect your thoughts and emotions: It's best to be calm when correcting an employee. If you're too excited, then you might blurt out something that will make matters worse. In addition, your employee might react badly to your anger or fear. It might turn into a shouting match or into an exchange of accusations. It's far better if you take the time to get yourself under control and decide what you will be saying. It's hard to control the situation when your own thoughts and feelings are running wild.

Time to gather evidence and documentation: You'll want to have any paperwork ready, like the Performance Improvement Notice form. You'll also want to gather any other documentation you'll need to explain the problem. When disciplining an employee for tardiness I had a list of the days they were late and by how much time. When disciplining an employee for inferior work, I had examples to show. Having the facts on-hand helps to make this more than a difference of opinions, it supports your words with facts.

Choose the Best Moment

Meet your employee on your terms, when *you're ready* and have all the necessary documentation. Beyond that, I'll offer only four other suggestions:

1. **Meet during work hours**. An employee should be disciplined on-the-clock. This is a work issue and should be resolved at work, not before they clock in or during their lunch break. This isn't something to do after hours either, unless you're planning to pay overtime for the 20 minutes or hour that you're meeting. Now the meeting might not be on company premises- it rarely was for me since I mainly supervised field personnel that were located in different cities and states- but the meeting should still happen while the employee is on-the-clock.

2. **Meet as soon as possible**. It is best to discipline an employee as soon as possible after the offense. Fresh is better- the employee will have a better memory of what happened and will more likely understand the connection between the problem and the correction you're enforcing. Wait too long it everything goes stale- the offense won't seem as vivid and the punishment might feel more vindictive to the employee. Also, waiting to discipline means that the employee might continue making the same errors and compound the problem their creating. So, as soon as you are ready, call for that disciplinary meeting. Don't delay.

3. **Choose a time when interruptions will be minimal**. You don't want a disciplinary meeting to drag out because of constant interruptions, so pick a time when intrusions will be less likely. You know the workflow at your business. Is there a time during the typical workday when things are quieter, like in the morning or during the afternoon lull? If so, then that would be the optimum time to take your employee away from his or her work and talk to them. Maybe you'll wait until another supervisor is back from lunch and can cover your calls. Maybe you'll need to appoint an office person to handle your calls while you're in the meeting. The idea is to take a moment, beforehand, to reduce the chance of interruptions during your disciplinary meeting. You'll want to pick the best time or create the best time for a disturbance-free meeting.

4. **Employee Availability**. When would be the best time to pull your employee away from his or her regular tasks? Done at the wrong time, your disciplinary meeting could interrupt the workflow of other employees, so pick a time when the problem employee will not be critically missed. Is your problem employee a part-timer or on a dynamic schedule? If so, you'll need to find out when they will be around for a disciplinary meeting. Will you need to find someone to substitute for your employee while the two of you are meeting? Just make sure the person you're disciplining is available and

that pulling them aside won't cause bigger problems.

Choose Meeting Length

Another issue that can arise is the never-ending disciplinary meeting. Sometimes, an employee will want to keep talking, explaining, or arguing. You should give an employee the opportunity to tell their side of the story, but it needs to be within limits. It's good to decide beforehand how much time you want to commit to this meeting. Most disciplinary meetings that I've held have lasted less than 20 minutes They usually dealt with straight-forward discipline, but some included termination as well. I've had meetings that were as short as 5 minutes, but those were usually verbal warnings where the employee and I were in full agreement about what went wrong and how to correct it. I've also had some lengthy meetings that involved serious allegations and witnesses, but those were rare. I prefer succinct meetings, which I've found to be best for me and for the employee.

Be assertive in controlling the meeting's length. Here are some ways to do so:

- **Write an outline of what you want to discuss**. Before the meeting you can create a list of what you want to cover and how much time you want to give each topic, that way you can make sure you cover everything and also you can refer to the outline to make sure you are getting to everything in a timely manner.

- **Schedule something afterward**. If you are prone to chat too long or to letting your employees ramble, you might want to force yourself to keep to a time limit by scheduling something afterward and letting your employee know that you'll need to finish this before that other thing starts.

- **Set a timer**. Most managers won't need to do this, but it might be necessary to set a timer on your phone or computer if you are prone to lose track of time or if your employee is one who loves to ramble.

- **Ask someone to call or interrupt your meeting at a certain**

time. This is a planned interruption to force the end of a meeting.

Overall, you should control the timing of your meeting: from start time to length. Control the *when* of your meeting to make it more effective.

Eric Lorenzen

CHAPTER TWELVE

Where: Control the Location

"Location, location, location."
- Anonymous real estate saying

Whenever possible, it is best to discipline an employee away from customers and other employees. You'll want to do this for two reasons: to prevent interruptions and to respect your employee.

In the previous chapter, we talked about the reasons for picking the best time for your disciplinary meeting, but here I want to talk about the importance of controlling the *location*. As much as possible, you'll want your meeting to be distraction-free and that won't happen by accident, so be pro-active in controlling where you'll meet and how that location is prepared. Do things in advance, like:

1. Tell your boss that you'll be in this meeting so that he or she will less likely interrupt
2. Set your phone on silence
3. If you have an assistant, have them run interference while the meeting happens

4. Arrange with another manager to cover your assigned area while you're in the meeting
5. Assign someone to handle customer questions and complaints for the duration
6. Make sure you don't have any scheduling conflicts that might cut your disciplinary meeting too short
7. If you're using a room that isn't often used, check to make sure the temperature and lighting is acceptable beforehand
8. If you're using your office, put away any sensitive data you don't want the employee seeing and clear a seat for them
9. Turn off your email alerts or silence them so that you won't be distracted and look away from your employee

With a little forethought, you can make this disciplinary meeting so much smoother. This isn't something you want to stretch out because of interruptions and distractions. Prepare, so that you can stay focused on your employee and can get this meeting done relatively quickly.

Know your Location

You should be the one to pick where a disciplinary meeting will be held. Be pro-active and pick a location that will work for you. I've held disciplinary meetings in a private office, a conference room, outside in a parking lot, at a restaurant, and in a quiet corner of a store. All of these settings had something in common: each place allowed me to talk in relative privacy as I disciplined the employee.

Every manager reading this book has a different work setting to deal with. Some will be working in an office, some in a retail store, and some supervise at a different job site daily. No matter the setting, the idea when it comes to disciplining an employee is to *pull aside*, to take them away from others and have a semi-private talk. While getting ready to discipline someone, you should take a moment and decide on the location even while you're getting everything else ready- like your PIN and any accompanying documentation.

Some things to consider when choosing your meeting location:

1. **Noise Level**: Will the two of you be able to hear each other? Hard to do that when too close to loud machinery, screaming kids, rushing highway traffic, blaring speakers, etc. I doubt that shouting to be heard is what either of you want. At the other extreme, you really don't want a setting where both of you are forced to whisper to keep from being overheard or from disturbing others. Pick a place where the two of you can talk in a normal voice.

2. **Seating**: It is perfectly fine to do a disciplinary meeting while standing, but if you're planning to sit down while doing this then there should be another chair available to your employee as well.

3. **Location Availability**: Will your chosen location be available when you need it and for the duration you want? A breakroom is quiet during the first two hours of a workday, but then other employees start wandering in for their rest period or early lunch. Similar timing problems could exist with a conference room, a restaurant booth, or even a shared office. Make sure the spot you pick is available for the time you need it.

Other Things to Consider

When you're deciding on the timing and location of your disciplinary meeting, please consider the following as well:

Discipline in Person. It's rarely acceptable to try disciplining through text or email. Written words can be easily misunderstood because they don't capture the nuances in your voice. If this is a disciplinary warning, it should be done in person.

When supervising remote employees you may be forced to discipline over the phone, but that should be a last resort. Consider a video link for the meeting instead, because then the two of you can see and hear each other, which will greatly improve the communication.

Privacy Preferred. In a disciplinary meeting you are dealing with sensitive personnel issues, so you will want to conduct this out of earshot of co-workers and customers. Would you want others listening in if you were being rebuked for poor performance? I think your answer would be "no" and your employee most likely wouldn't want that either. If you want to turn this employee's performance and attitude around, then offer them the dignity of a non-public meeting. Otherwise, you will likely embarrass or anger them, for they will see your actions as a public shaming.

It is understood that sometimes you don't have the luxury of getting that employee away from others. Sometimes you must discipline immediately, like when you see someone doing something dangerous or destructive- you yell out *stop!* or *watch out!* no matter who might overhear you. But usually, you can pull that employee aside to discipline them without shaming them in front of everyone else.

Visibility is Also Preferred. When holding a disciplinary meeting, it also best to hold it where others can see you without overhearing. Open curtains in a room or leave a door open. Pick a corner of the warehouse away from everyone else but still within sight. Why? This is done as a precaution, for your safety and to protect your reputation. This may never happen to you, but should an employee become violent during a meeting others can quickly intervene. Another rare occurrence is the employee who makes false claims about your meeting. Should an employee claim that you touched them inappropriately (either in anger or in lust), the fact that you met somewhere visible to others will help disprove such outrageous lies. Most likely, you'll never face either a fistfight or a sexual harassment claim, but why not take a little bit of extra effort to make sure your meeting is in a location where others can at least glimpse in?

Adding a Witness

There will be times when you'll want at witness for a disciplinary meeting. You'll want someone else there to hear the stories from both sides, especially if you fear that the employee might become enraged or might add to his or her misdeeds by lying or accusing you of misbehavior during the meeting. Some worry that charges of harassment, discrimination, bigotry, or racism might be claimed against them, especially if the employee has made such accusations against others before. If faced with such a scenario, it can be wise to have someone else there to witness the meeting.

The question then arises of who to add in as a witness. Because this is a personnel issue, it should be treated as a confidential meeting by anyone attending. You don't want your witness gossiping about what they heard at a disciplinary meeting. That is why you should enlist another supervisor to join you. Presumably, the other manager would already understand the importance of discretion.

If you must have an hourly employee as a witness, try to get someone who isn't working every day with the employee you're disciplining. That's not always possible, especially in a small company, but try your best. At bigger companies they often have someone from the Human Resources department join in on disciplinary meetings but smaller businesses often don't have an in-house HR person, so pick a seasoned hourly employee or one who works in a different area to serve as your witness during your meeting.

Eric Lorenzen

CHAPTER THIRTEEN
HOW:
Control Your
Empathy

"Faithful are the wounds of a friend; but the kisses of an enemy are deceitful."
- Proverbs 27:6 KJV

One of the traits of great managers is the ability to understand your employees- to have empathy with them during their ups and downs. Employees usually appreciate a supervisor who takes the time to get to know them and who understands the circumstances in their lives. That empathy can be very helpful during your normal daily interactions with an employee, but it can really complicate things when disciplining.

When you need to confront a problem you will need to control your empathy, not shutting it off but channeling it in the right direction. Direct your empathy toward helping your employee succeed at their job, and they cannot succeed if they aren't confronted with their errors and have the chance to correct them. Empathy that tries to hide the employee's problems isn't empathy at all; it's really cruelty. When you don't help an employee deal with their shortcomings it simply postpones that confrontation and often allows the problems to grow into a much bigger issue. Your misplaced kindness ends up causing greater damage.

Stop Sabotaging Your Authority

In some situations, a manager can feel terrible about being the "meanie" at work, the one who breaks up the fun and demands that people get to work. But that's your job. If you can't do it, then resign. You are expected to make sure the "job gets done" and that everyone does their part. It can be even harder when an employee has a sob story for not keeping up to company standards. When tempted to be overly lenient, consider these three stops:

Stop Acting like a Buddy. You might feel like a "friend" to your employee, but during a disciplinary action is not the time to show that. (See Chapter Seven, *No Excuses from You* for more discussion on the Curse of the Best Buddy) Your disciplinary meeting will quickly turn into an awkward mess if you insist on acting like best buddies during the meeting. Now is the time to be professional and stick to the facts. The employee errored and now they need to face that fact and that they need to improve. An attempt to be a buddy in the midst of this will muddle your message.

Stop Acting like a Therapist. Remember the reason why you are meeting. You don't want your disciplinary meeting to turn into a pseudo counseling session. You are not their therapist or marriage counselor or doctor. Remember who you are; you are their supervisor. Resist the desire to offer life advice or to become a confidante. If you need to act like a counselor or a confessional priest, please do so away from work.

Stop Acting like Nothing is Wrong. This isn't actually empathy, but some managers convince themselves that they are being caring by not confronting the issue. Most likely, this is really a fear of confrontation (See Chapter Seven, *No Excuses from You* for more discussion on the need to confront employees). Ignoring the problem is not a way to be nice to your employee. What you are actually doing is sabotaging their future at that job and any other they might have. How can they improve as a worker if they never learn that their actions (or inaction) are causing problems? You are also sabotaging your own career by ignoring things that need to be dealt with.

Start Caring by Doing Your Job

If you really want to be a caring boss, then you need to be one of integrity and transparency. It's about more than just being nice-employees want a supervisor who is truthful, straight-forward, and fair. Truly caring is doing these things:

Start Caring by Being Honest. You need to be honest with your employees. Pretending that a problem doesn't exist or lying and saying it really isn't a problem does nothing for you, for the employee, or for the team. Obviously, this issue is enough of a problem that you're holding a disciplinary meeting, so don't waffle on it. It is selfish to avoid confrontation by ignoring the problem while it just grows worse. Be truthful with your employee and let them know this is a problem that they need to correct. By doing that you are being caring, because that employee has no chance to improve if they don't know how serious the issue is. If you care, you will share the truth.

Start Caring by Being Clear. The best way to be a caring boss is to be clear about the problem and providing a path to improvement. It is selfish on your part to muddy things up by turning a disciplinary meeting into something else. It's selfish to withhold the specifics because you don't want to get into the ugly details. It's selfish to downplay the problem and act as if it isn't as bad as it truly is. Selfishness isn't being very caring toward your employees. Your employee deserves clarity from you. Your employee deserves to know if there's a problem, or else they will have no idea that they need to improve at something. If you care, you'll be straight-forward with them.

Start Caring by Being Consistent. The hardest kind of boss to have is an inconsistent boss- someone who changes their standards and expectations daily or even hourly. Don't let your moods change your standards. Just because you're happy today, doesn't mean you should let all the mistakes slip past you. Just because you're mad or moody today, doesn't mean you should crack the whip on the slightest hint of an error. Instead, strive to keep up the same standards every day, every month, every year. When you're consistent you're being fair to everyone, and that reveals that really do care.

Empathy Controlled

Good managers care for their employees, but those emotions are controlled in a way that helps both the employees and the business. Your feelings shouldn't be leading you to neglect or indulge your staff. Instead, your feelings should be pushing you to be a better boss: fair to all, clear in your directions, and honest with anyone who messes up. Acting this way might not come easy for you, but it's worth it. Act this way and you can earn the respect of your employees, and then they will likely work harder and have more job satisfaction.

CHAPTER FOURTEEN
What:
Control the
Conversation

*"Concentration is the secret of strength in politics, in war, in trade,
in short in all the management of human affairs."*
- Ralf Waldo Emerson

Out of respect for yourself and your employee, keep any disciplinary meeting professional and on-topic. Over the years, I've encountered so many different ways that a disciplinary meeting can get detoured. At times I was the guilty party, letting myself wander off the trail so-to-speak. Other times, it was the employee who tried to talk about other things. None of that is helpful. For a disciplinary meeting to be successful, you need to keep it centered on the right things. That doesn't just happen by accident; it takes work on the part of a manager to keep the meeting heading in the right direction.

Of course a good manager doesn't turn a disciplinary meeting into a berating lecture where the employee needs to silently cower, so your control shouldn't smother all discussion. This is a conversation between two adults in an attempt to understand and correct something the employee is doing wrong.

You want to control the conversation for at least three reasons:

- **Clarity**. You don't want this to become confusing or muddled. By controlling the conversation you can keep out the unimportant.

- **Focus**. The employee is more likely to understand the problem if the only things you talk about are your current concerns with this particular employee, instead of side issues, concerns with others, or past problems.

- **Results**. There's a better chance the employee will improve if they understand the importance of the issue and your expectations of change.

Conversation is Two-Sided and Purposeful

A disciplinary meeting should be a conversation as opposed to a lecture. Both parties should talk and respond. However, this isn't just an aimless chat; it is purposeful. There is a reason for this meeting, a topic for this conversation, and that is your employee's behavior or job performance. When both parties are involved and discussing, then it will more likely result in change.

Listen to your employee. No matter what mistakes they made, they deserve to be heard. You might not agree with what they say, but listen anyways. A disciplinary meeting is much more successful when both participate rather than just a lecture from you, so let the employee share too.

Try to get them to talk. Sometimes an employee would rather just listen passively and maybe nod their head. That doesn't mean they agree with you; they may just be wanting this meeting to end as fast as possible. If you can, get them to share their side of the story. If they are still silent, then at least have them repeat back to you what changes you are expecting to happen. You can't force them to converse, but they should at least give an audible acknowledgment to what you're saying.

Keep it purposeful. Finally, do your part to guide the conversation. As stated above, you want this to be clear, focused, and to bring results. To bring that about, you'll need to *exert control* during a meeting.

Controlling Your Part of the Conversation

If you want this to be successful at disciplining an employee, you'll need to control the direction of the meeting, control what you're saying, and control how it ends. Don't leave it up to chance, but be proactive in making sure this meeting conveys your concerns and what you expect to change.

To help do this, consider the following points:

- **Write an outline of what you want to discuss.** Before the meeting you may want to create a list of the points to cover so that you can refer back and make sure you are keeping the meeting on-topic. If nothing else, keep the PIN in front of you and refer back often to make sure you talk about all the points you have written down.

- **Limit the topics of your meeting.** You might have a lot of things that you'd like to talk with this employee about, but keep it to the most important ones, the true problems that this disciplinary meeting is meant to address. This is not the time to talk about new initiatives, schedule changes, upcoming client meetings, or any of a hundred other subjects. Save those side issues for another time or else this will turn into a long and confusing meeting.

- **Don't drag up the past unless it's directly connected.** Avoid bringing up past infringements and mistakes if they happened long ago or aren't relevant to this particular problem. To do so might confuse the employee or make them resentful- you're bringing up something that they thought had already been resolved a long time ago. Keep it to the current issue and leave off rehashing old history.

- **Be sure to end with a call-to-action.** Talking about what's wrong is important but it's not enough. You need to end any disciplinary meeting with directions on what the employee must do to improve. They need a clear call-to-action or else they might not know how to fix the problem. Thankfully, if you're using a PIN like the example in this book, it will naturally lead you to ending with the steps the employee will need to take to improve.

Controlling the Direction of Your Employee's Conversation

Another problem that can arise is the employee who wants to talk about other things besides what this meeting is about. You'll want to let your employee share, but sometimes you'll need to redirect them to the topic at-hand, which is their misdeed or shortcoming.

Be assertive in controlling the meeting's topics. Here are some ways to do so:

- **Keep bringing it back to the problem**. Sometimes you'll need to work hard to stop your employee from going off on tangents and complaints that really have nothing to do with the problem you're discussing. Keep pointing them back to the issue at-hand.

- **Limit their time for excuses and explanations.** You should give your employee the opportunity to explain their side of the story, but it needs to be within limits. Don't let them keep going on and on, even repeating themselves. Politely yet firmly redirect back to the problem, to what happened (no matter what excuses they give) and how you want to see it change.

- **Cut short talk about others**. Keep it focused on this employee and what they did. Maybe others have messed up too, but this isn't about them. Explain that you keep personnel matters confidential, so you can't talk about other people right now. This is about what *this employee* did or didn't do.

- **Cut short attempts to blame you**. Some employees might try to turn-the-tables on you and claim that the real problem is you. You weren't clear. You should have warned them earlier. You didn't train them enough. You should be paying them better. You're a lousy manager. Don't let them turn this into an argument about whether you did your job or not. It's not their responsibility to determine if you're a good manager, especially not at this moment. Yes, it's best to own up to any mistakes on your part, but force the conversation back onto them. They failed at something, no matter the excuse. The standards should have been clear and they fell short of those standards, so that's why they are getting disciplined.

- **Have the employee acknowledge your expectations**. They need to admit that they heard you. No matter how much the employee disagrees with what you are saying in a disciplinary meeting, you should insist that they acknowledge an understanding of what you are asking them to change. They need to admit that they understand what you want, whether they agree with it or not. They need to admit what actions are expected from them to avoid further disciplinary action.

What Should be Said in a Meeting

I've held hundreds of disciplinary meetings and all of them were different- different people, different issues, different attitudes, different responses. However, all the meetings that were successful kept to a basic outline:

1. This is the problem/ issue
2. These are the details of that problem/issue
3. This is what you need to do to correct the problem/ issue
4. These are the consequences if it doesn't get corrected
5. Do you understand what is expected of you to get this right?

That is why a disciplinary form (like the sample PIN in this book) is great to have on hand, because it provides much of this outline right in front of you. Make sure to address all the points on the above outline and the meeting will be far more successful.

Eric Lorenzen

CHAPTER FIFTEEN
Show the Way

"Hear counsel, and receive instruction,
that thou mayest be wise in thy latter end."
- Proverbs 19:20 KJV

As a homeowner, it's frustrating when I know there's a problem but I don't know how to fix it. I'm not the best DIYer, so I've had my share of electrical or plumbing issues that I knew needed fixing but I had no clue on how to do it. Thankfully, I've often found tutorial videos online for those issues and can then try to fix the problem. Unfortunately, an employee usually can't search on Google for the specifics on how to improve a particular problem at work. They are dependent on us- their boss- to show them what they need to do to get it right. They need us to show them the way.

A disciplinary meeting without direction is just a gripe session. Pointing out the problem is only half of the process; showing the way to improvement is the other half. "Don't do that again" works for some discipline issues but not for most. For your employee to succeed you need to show them what they need to do/ change/ correct. That's common sense, but often we as managers can skimp on this vital step. To us, it seems so obvious what has to change but that might not be the case for the employee. We can't assume they will instantly know what they need to change to meet company standards. We need to clearly state our expectations of change. Don't just tell them they're doing something wrong; tell them what's the right thing to do.

Be Clear that They Can Improve

If you want to keep an employee that you're disciplining, you'll need to show them that it isn't hopeless. They need to know that there is a way to get this right. Even if you think the odds are against them and that they probably won't reform, you need to give them a fair chance. I'm not talking about lowering the expectations or any special exemptions, but you need to at least offer them the opportunity to get it right (in most cases- obviously some offenses don't deserve anything except an immediate firing).

You're employee might be in the deep, dark Valley of Lousy Performance but you need to be fair enough to at least point out where they need to be, up there on Mount Good Job. You might have your doubts that they will be able to make that steep climb and do it in two days, but it would be wrong to refuse to even point out the goal, to not even bother to let them know that there is a higher place where they ought to be.

Be Clear on How to Improve

Every employee deserves to know the *path to improvement*, a way that they can correct this particular problem and allow them to become a better employee. That path will differ depending on the offense, so you need to clearly show it to your employee.

Some paths are short. It might be "don't wear shorts to work," or maybe it's "be here at 8am sharp and ready to work," or maybe it's "always answer the phone with our company greeting." These are all short paths that are easy to show, even if it might be an effort for the employee to improve (buying new clothes, setting their morning alarm to go off an hour earlier, breaking the habit of answering the phone with just a "hello"). As long as they understand what they need to change, it's up to them to determine how they can accomplish the change. I'm not going to be the one to decide if they need to go to bed earlier or if they need to set their alarm to go off at 6:22 every morning- the exact steps are up to them as long as they clearly see the path they need to take to improve. My job is to illuminate the path and make it

106

clear to them; their job is to actually walk that path. When it's a short path, the employee should be able to see the way to improvement with minimal direction. Just be clear in pointing it out.

Other paths to success are longer or more involved. For example, if poor work quality were the issue, then improving could involve memorizing multiple steps done in a particular sequence. You may need to offer your employee detailed directions on how to navigate the path to meeting company standards. But whatever is needed, you should provide clear directions on how to accomplish what is required of them. I'm not saying that we need to give them a piggyback ride or even hold their hand along the whole route- they need to walk the path to improvement on their own- but we should offer them clear directions along a path that we have clearly marked. That's only fair on our part.

Be Realistic with Improvement Goals

Don't set improvement goals that no normal person could ever reach. If you're demanding the impossible, the employee won't even try. *Impossible standards* are something a normal worker could never attain. No even the world's best baseball player could "bat a thousand" for long; even the best employee will make mistakes and under-perform at times. So consider whether your "steps for improvement" for this employee are realistic. Are these requirements even doable for a typical employee?

Now don't confuse impossible standards with an employee who finds it impossible to meet the standards. As long as the standards are realistic and fair, the onus of meeting those standards falls on the employee. If he or she cannot meet them, then they need to be further reprimanded, demoted, or even fired.

Be Open to Alternative Routes to the Same Goals

If your "actions to improve performance" look like the sheer face of Yosemite's Half Dome looming over your hapless employee, then you might be acting a little unrealistic in your expectations. If your employee has to make that huge of an improvement, you might need to offer some interim goals to meet on their climb to reaching company standards. No need to lower standards for them, but be realistic on how to get there. A person can still get to the top of Half Dome without scaling its vertical face- you can go around to the back and climb the steep steps with the help of steel cable guide-lines. Both routes require hard work and both get you to the top, but one is far more doable than the other.

Be open to possible other routes to reaching the same expected standards. Your employee might even suggest an alternative way that makes more sense. You should even be willing to rewrite that part of the PIN listing "actions to improve performance" if you find a better way. There's no need to budge on standards, just be willing to reconsider the way to attain those standards.

Be Realistic with Time Limits

"*I want change and I want it now!*" Demanding immediate correction is realistic with some types of issues, like dress code violations or failing to follow safety procedures. But other times, it might take weeks for an employee to improve. When dealing with work quality, work quantity, or work pace, it might take an employee time to rise up to the expected standards. They might need some practice or some mentoring to learn the right work speed or how to catch those flaws that cause work quality to suffer. So be realistic in the time limits you set for them to improve.

"*Some day you'll need to do better at this.*" I've never said that to any employee that I've disciplined, and that's because I can't let them set their own pace. It can't be open-ended, letting the employee choose when they will start improving or how fast they will improve. Being realistic with time limits doesn't mean an employee can take their own sweet time to mossy along the path to improvement. Being realistic means that you set clear goals that are attainable within the time parameters you have set.

An Example of Improvement Steps

Cashier John is too slow as he checks out customers at a home improvement store, even after some additional training. He tends to chat too long with people, miss-scan items, and then needs to spend more time double-checking that he rang up everything. When you hold the disciplinary meeting about his unacceptable work pace, your "actions to improve performance" might look something like this:

1. Greet each customer but don't delay with distracting conversation. Ask them to place their items on the counter except the over-sized items.

2. Ask the customer to turn large items (like 5 gallon buckets of paint and longer lumber pieces) still in their cart so that you can scan the bar codes. While they are doing that you can start scanning merchandise on the counter.

3. Concentrate on the items you are scanning, making sure the bar code is turned the right way. You should be scanning each item once, not two or three times because it's turned the wrong way.

4. Bag each item immediately to prevent confusion of whether you scanned it or not.

5. Use the hand scanner to ring-up any larger items. That should go quickly because the customer has already turned the bar codes out. Pay attention as you scan so that you don't miss-scan or forget anything.

6. Be friendly but complete the sale quickly, without any unnecessary chatting. You need to get to the next customer as quickly as possible.

Frankly, this can probably be reduced to an even tighter list of actions, depending on how well the employee understands his job as a cashier, but I think you get the idea. It offers clear directions and mentions the areas where Cashier John is slowing down or having to redo his work. Considering the depth of the action list, I would guess that Cashier John is still new at the job- for you wouldn't have to be so detailed with a veteran cashier.

Show the Way during every Disciplinary Meeting

If you want a great team of employees working for you, then you'll work hard to show them how to get the job done well and quickly. That's part of the daily job of a manager, and it is even more vital to continue showing the way during a disciplinary meeting. Not only do they need to know what's wrong, they need to know what's right.

Clearly show your employee how they can do better and they will have a much greater chance at succeeding.

Your
Follow-up

Eric Lorenzen

CHAPTER SIXTEEN

Follow-Up, Direction, and Praise

"Correction does much, but encouragement does more."
- Johann Wolfgang Von Goethe

The bane of all managers is their own busyness. It's so easy to let things fall through the cracks, like returning a call or getting back to someone with an answer that you have to research. Following up on a disciplinary meeting can also fall victim to our busyness. Truthfully, it can be one of the hardest things for a manager to do consistently. However, it is vital to provide follow-up and further communication with that employee.

Have they improved?
- They need to hear that.
Are they making progress but aren't quite there yet?
- Let them know and encourage them to keep going.
Have you seen no change whatsoever?
- Well, that needs to be dealt with too.
You need to check back, maybe in a week or maybe in a month,

and see if the employee has improved. Do they now meet or even surpass company standards? You can't assume that all will be well just because you had a disciplinary meeting. You need to verify that the employee has indeed corrected the problem.

When an employee shows improvement, you need to encourage them. They will be far more motivated by your sincere praise than they will be by your discipline alone.

Follow-up with Praise

When an employee has shaped-up, you need to recognize the change. It can sometimes be easy to overlook an employee who has improved and now is meeting standards. They're no longer an issue so they no longer catch your attention, but don't forget to let them know you've seen the difference in their work performance. Take the time to praise.

While you discipline in private, you can certainly praise in public. It doesn't hurt to tell an employee they're doing a good job in front of others. Not only will it give the employee a sense of pride in their performance, it will often encourage others to work harder too. But you don't have to talk to them in front of everyone; you can also pull the employee aside to praise their improvement and to encourage them to keep going.

Be just as purposeful with your praise as you are with correction. When an employee who was disciplined about a shortcoming is now doing much better, you need to recognize it by speaking up. If their attitude has improved or if they're being more careful or if their work pace is much faster, let them know that you've notice the change. By praising their improvement, you are reinforcing their better behavior. You are giving them another reason to try harder.

Follow-up with More Direction

What if an employee is steadily improving but isn't up to standards yet? Most often, I would encourage them to keep at it and give them some more direction on how to make it happen. As long as

114

the employee is making decent progress at a satisfactory pace, I usually wouldn't resort to another disciplinary meeting. However, if they are making progress but it's taking too much time, I might have to talk with them again.

There may be times when you'll need to modify how you're following up on an employee. You might need to be more proactive, giving them specific interim goals and detailed instructions because they need more guidance. Unless it's too much of a burden, do what it takes to get your employee up-to-standards. That extra effort on your part could save them from "almost making it." Why just passively watch them flounder if a little extra effort on your part can help them succeed?

Follow-up with Further Discipline

When an employee fails to improve, it's time for more consequences. I can't just ignore it nor can I put it off because I'm too busy. In addition, the next step shouldn't be lighter than the first one I took. If I've already written them up for this problem, I'm not going to step-it-down to just a verbal warning this time. The employee will get a second written warning at minimum. No matter what's going on at work or how busy we are, if the employee still isn't meeting company standards, then I need to discipline them again. It might mean a second Verbal Warning, a Written Warning, or even a Suspension. In a worst case scenario, it will mean termination of employment. The idea of Progressive Discipline is that the discipline progresses to a harsher punishment if there isn't satisfactory improvement.

If you used the PIN example from this book, then you've already spelled out what will happen, having written it in the section titled "Next Disciplinary Step if Performance Does Not Improve." Now is the time to follow through with the warning you gave them when had that first disciplinary meeting. Show that you are a manager of your word, by following through with what you said would happen.

What if the employee is trying but not succeeding? For me, this is a much harder scenario than the employee who just doesn't bother to try. When an employee is making a sincere effort but it's still unacceptable, it forces me to make a hard choice. Keeping a mediocre employee will hurt productivity and work quality. In addition, keeping that person might discourage the rest of the team and damage customer relations. Considering all those serious consequences, I then have to ask myself questions like: Is there any hope that this employee will ever reach our standards? Can they be shifted to another job? Would their performance be acceptable if they worker fewer hours with less responsibilities? Is it time to look for a replacement? I need to consider all those possibilities and then decide what to do with this mediocre employee. A well-meaning but still lousy employee is harder to fire, but sometimes I'll still have to terminate them.

What if a once-good employee can no longer meet company standards? Maybe they were good at one time, but now their performance is greatly diminished. Maybe they can't keep up with the new, faster pace. Maybe they can't adjust to new technology or new techniques. Maybe company standards were raised and the employee can't meet the new level. There can be so many reasons why a once-good employee is no longer meeting standards. Depending on the reason, you're response might differ.

You'll need to determine if it's worth trying to salvage this employee. If their performance is now awful because of a change in their attitude, then I wouldn't bother keeping them. If their performance isn't good enough due to physical limitations (like age or health), it might be worth considering a new role for them where they are doing more supervision or mentoring of the less-experienced. In that way, you are still tapping into their superior knowledge and experience while lightening the physical burden of the job. Another possible solution if the employee has an issue with stamina is moving them to part-time status. If you think the employee is salvageable and you have the flexibility to offer some kind of alternative, then it might be worth talking to them and see if you can find something that will be satisfactory to both of you.

Tricks to Remembering to Follow-Up

No matter what, you need to follow-up on any employee that you've disciplined. You need to be purposeful about this or you might forget, so find whatever works for you and do it.

Pick your follow-up day(s) right after you finish doing a disciplinary meeting. You've just completed your meeting and are gathering up your notes and getting ready to put the PIN in the employee's personnel file. Take a moment to pick the day(s) when you will check on your employee's progress. For some violations, like dress code or safety procedures, it might be checking as soon as tomorrow and then once more in two weeks. For other issues, it might mean checking once a week for the next month. Other problems might require a follow-up in 30 days. Some employees might need to be checked on once, while others might need multiple reviews to make sure they're showing adequate improvement. You decide what makes the most sense for you but decide it now, at the conclusion of your meeting, before you get busy with other things. Look at the calendar and note what day(s) will work. You don't need to talk about any of this with your employee, but some managers do. The important thing is to get the follow-up date(s) onto your calendar now.

Create reminders for yourself. Note the follow-up date(s) on your schedule or calendar. Put a reminder alarm on your phone for that date. Do whatever is necessary to make sure the date doesn't slip past you and suddenly days, weeks, or even months have gone by and you haven't checked on your employee's progress.

Eric Lorenzen

CHAPTER SEVENTEEN
Termination
Requirements

"Extreme remedies are very appropriate for extreme diseases."
- Hippocrates, *Aphorisms*

It's practically guaranteed that you'll terminate at least a few people during your career as a manager, and some of those terminations will be involuntary ones- a firing. Obviously, an involuntary termination is the extreme end of discipline, but sometimes that is what's necessary. An employee's extreme actions (or inactions) require the ultimate response.

Knowing that you will most likely need to terminate someone some day, you might as well be ready for it. When it comes time to terminate, you want to be prepared to do it succinctly and correctly. In this chapter we'll talk about the steps involved and some of the laws to consider.

Most veteran managers have fired their share of employees. If that manager is from a high-turnover industry, they might have fired so many that they couldn't even give you an exact number. Instead, they'll talk about the dozens or even hundreds that they've terminated over the years. I certainly can't give you more than a rough estimate. If we're talking about employees who I've fired, the count will be in the dozens. If we're talking how many people I've taken through the termination procedures (which also includes those laid-off and those who voluntarily quit), the number jumps to hundreds. The numbers aren't something to brag about, but neither should we be embarrassed. It's just reality.

In this chapter we will look at the different types of terminations and some of the legal requirements you may have to consider.

Three Types of Terminations

Employment is terminated for 3 reasons:

1. **The Employee Quits**. This is considered a "voluntary quit" and is usually the main cause of turnover. The employee decides to end their own employment. Some quit because they see the "writing on the wall" and realize that you are close to firing them anyway- which spares you the hassle. Many quit because they don't want to work there anymore. They might leave for another job, to go back to school, or to move to a different area. The reasons why they've chosen to leave will vary with the person and most won't tell you the full story of why they're leaving. Often, the employee will blame you (at least partially) as the cause of their leaving, so face that fact whether it's justified or not.

   i) **Some quit passively**- they just stop showing up and abandon the job. When someone just disappears like that, it leaves you in uncertainty. Are they just too sick to call in? Were they in a car accident? It might take you a few days or even weeks to find out what has really happened. You'll be calling them and, if that doesn't work, the emergency contact numbers on file. It will be frustrating and maybe even worrisome until you find out the truth- which is usually that the person decided to take a different job or has moved to a different city and just didn't bother to tell you. **Job abandonment** is considered a "voluntary termination" unless the employee is somehow incapacitated and unable to notify you (like being in intensive care at a local hospital). Many company's define job abandonment in their policies as a set length (often stated as 3 days of no-show and no-contact), which provides clarity to everyone. If they miss three consecutive days of work without contacting the company it is considered quitting.

ii) **Most tell you that they are quitting**. They might tell you on-the-spot- "*I Quit!*"- and then storm out the door. They might give you a month's notice, giving you ample time to start looking for a replacement. No matter if they give you notice or not, it is very clear that their employment is ending and it is their choice. If they gave advance notice you aren't required to let them work that long. Sometimes it might be necessary to cut short that window of two-weeks or a month because the employee is slacking off or causing trouble, so you turn their voluntary quit into a firing. Don't let them linger at the job if they are sabotaging things for you or the team.

2. **The Employee gets Laid Off**. For me, these were the hardest terminations to do, because the employees hadn't done anything deserving of termination- it was just a business decision. Sometimes you have to reduce staff due to lost revenue or the need to shrink staffing. Other times, the lay-off is triggered by a pivot in the business (we have a new direction, new focus) that has made their job obsolete or duplicative. A lay-off is considered an "involuntary termination," so you should review the section below that mentions paycheck laws and the WARN Act.

3. **The Employee is Fired**. You are firing this person because they haven't improved after numerous warning or because they've done something so egregious that they need to be let go. This is reserved for employees that 1) are already causing problems while still in their introductory period, 2) continue to repeat offenses that they have be written up for, 3) have too many write-ups for various topics, or 4) have committed a

particularly bad offense such as theft or sexual harassment.

Constraints on Firing

Labor laws are complex and change every year. The laws differ by state, city, business size, and industry, and that is just here in the USA. This book is not meant to be a comprehensive guide to the possible legal ramifications you might face- please consult a competent professional in your area if you need legal advice. That being said, here are a few areas that a manager should always consider when getting ready to terminate someone.

Are you an At-Will employer? Most states in the USA allow private employers to offer at-will employment, which means that a person's employment can be terminated by either the employer or the employee, with or without cause or advanced notice. Most companies seem to prefer being at-will employers and establish that fact in all their formal correspondence with their staff, from hiring letters to employee handbooks.

Companies endanger that at-will status when they use employee contracts or insist that an employee must give advanced notice before quitting. Even worse are the employers who claim that you can't quit until you train your replacement. Just realize that at-will employment is not one-sided; it's an "open relationship" for both parties where either side can end it immediately.

If you are not an at-will employer, then you will probably be restrained to only firing with cause.

Another point of note: we aren't talking about Unemployment Benefits here. That is a whole different can of worms that I won't pry open, beyond noting that whether an ex-employee will be granted unemployment benefits is determined by other factors, such as whether this was a voluntary termination or an involuntary termination, and whether termination was for just cause or not.

Do any of your employees have an employment contract? If your company is unionized, then that union agreement obviously sets the parameters of any employee discipline or termination. Take the time to learn the procedures and limitations that were agreed to with the union. But even if your business is not unionized, there may be some employees that were hired under an employment contract. This is sometimes done with specialists that are in high-demand or with top executives as a way to woo them to join the team. The contract might guarantee a minimum length of employment among other things. If you are supervising someone that was hired under a contract, you should get to know the details of that contract to make sure it won't interfere with any need you might have to discipline or terminate the individual.

What are the paycheck laws for your region or business? Paycheck laws determine, among other things, deadlines when a person should get their final paycheck. These laws can differ by state or even by city. Your legal requirements probably also differ on whether this is a voluntary or an involuntary termination. In some states, you may need to issue the final paycheck to a fired employee within twenty-four hours of termination, while at the other extreme in some states the law allows you to wait until the next regular pay date to issue the final check to an employee who voluntarily quit. Take the time to familiarize yourself with the paycheck laws in your area so that you remain in compliance with such labor laws.

Final pay would usually include things like weekly salary, hourly wages, mileage allowances, earned vacation pay, earned PTO, and also earned commissions. Commissions can be a more complex item to calculate for that final paycheck and state laws differ and are often vague on how quickly they should be paid. You cannot deny earned commissions but you may have to delay until actual payment for a sale is received. (Check with a labor law professional for a definitive time frame for payout.)

Reimbursement of expenses, on the other hand, are not usually considered a part of final wages and can usually be delayed until proper paperwork is submitted by the employee, waiting until the next scheduled payout date. You are fine to insist that an employee submit all the necessary forms that they would usually be required to complete (such mileage reports and expense reports) before the company will reimburse those expenses.

Are there any advance notification requirements? Certain businesses (often due to their size) must provide advance warning (typically 60 days) if they are planning to lay off multiple employees at the same time. If you are planning to downsize personnel or relocating an office to another city or state, take the time to familiarize yourself with any applicable laws. At the US federal level, it is usually referred to as the WARN Act and mainly affects companies with 100 or more employees, but your state or city may have laws that pertain to smaller companies or even specific industries. Again, these particular laws are about mass lay-offs as opposed to the termination of one or two individuals.

Fire as Needed, But Only as Needed

Most likely, you're business is an at-will employer, which means you can terminate employment with or without notice or cause. "With or Without Notice" means that you can give them advance notice (your job is ending in three months), but you don't have to. You can terminate without any advance notice and often when firing someone it will be immediate. "With or Without Cause" means that you can have a reason for firing someone but it isn't required. You don't have to explain your reasoning to the employee; you can just say that their employment is over.

However, being an at-will employer doesn't exempt you from the laws protecting employees from discrimination and harassment. If an employee can prove that you terminated them because of your sexism or ageism or bigotry or racism you are still liable for those legal consequences. That's why it's vital that you document any termination, showing for your own records why you terminated someone. For an involuntary termination you should have a good reason that is either for the good of the business (for a lay-off) or caused by the employee's poor performance or workplace behavior (for a firing). Document it, whether you explain it all to the employee or not.

In addition, be aware that your reasons for termination and your documentation could help determine whether that ex-employee will be awarded unemployment benefits or not.

There is no way to guarantee that you'll never be called to court because of a former employee, but if you document their misbehavior and the reasons behind their termination, you'll probably have an easier time defending your actions. Keep it focused on the work and not the worker.

How do you Fire?

Now that we've considered the different types of terminations and some of the legal requirements, it's time to look at how to actually terminate someone. In the next chapter we'll look at the steps to follow when firing an employee, from paperwork to escorting them off the premises.

Eric Lorenzen

CHAPTER EIGHTEEN

How to Fire

"Cast out the scorner, and contention shall go out;
yea, strife and reproach shall cease."
- Proverbs 22:10 KJV

Let's be blunt: some employees just need to be *cast out* of your business- thrown to the curb. They are troublemakers, scornful, or lazy butts. You are far better without them. Once gone, it will seem as if the strife and problems have finally ended.

Firing an employee is the ultimate step in discipline. It is the last resort because the employee cannot be salvaged. You don't necessarily fire someone because they made a huge mistake that cost the company tons of money- that employee might still be salvageable and could turn out to be a great asset to the business. It will up to you (and your supervisors) to decide if an employee's huge mess-up deserves a firing. Sometimes those big blunders result in getting fired, but many terminations are actually the result of an accumulation of smaller misdeeds and mistakes. The employee just keeps *coming up short* and there seems to be no hope for reform.

Some employees will never be good, whether it's because of their abilities or their attitude. You could spend months or years working with them, but they can't or won't meet company standards. Other times, an employee messes up so spectacularly that they don't deserve a second chance; their actions were just too egregious, like theft or sexual harassment. As a manager, you will need to fire them, whether it came up all-at-once or over time.

In this chapter, we will look at how to prepare for a termination and how to conduct that meeting.

Preparing for a Termination

In some companies, a manager must get the approval of their supervisor or an HR manager before firing anyone. Please be aware of what's required and follow those procedures. But even if you have the authority to terminate, you will still need to have some things ready before you actually fire anyone.

Paperwork: Before terminating an employee, you'll want to get certain paperwork ready:

- Termination Letter (see sample below)
- List of Company Property that they need to return (see section following)
- Final Paycheck probably (see previous chapter for comments about paycheck laws)
- Box for carrying out their personal items
- Instructions for Additional Paperwork (see right below)

The employee may need to submit additional paperwork for things like Expense Reports, Mileage Reimbursement, COBRA health insurance coverage, or 401(k) rollover. For reimbursement of mileage and approved expenses, most companies ask a terminated employee to submit all their required paperwork by the usual deadline to receive their payment. I'm not aware of any state laws setting a time limit of how quickly to reimburse a terminated employee for expenses outside of pay, but it shouldn't be delayed beyond the typical payout window. (As always when dealing with labor laws, I recommend checking in your area to confirm that they are no requirements of quicker reimbursements to terminated employees.)

Setting and Assistance: Much like a disciplinary meeting, you'll want to decide ahead of time *when* and *where* you want to terminate this person. What will be the best place to hold this brief meeting? When is the best time of day to do this? Because fired employees can get very emotional or even angry, it is often best not to do a termination in an isolated place or after all other employees have already left work. You might want to enlist a witness for the termination or someone to help assist in escorting the person off the premises. Most fired employees do not get violent, but take precautions as you deem necessary.

Securing People and Property

When getting ready to terminate an employee, you will need to consider quite a few things. Although it doesn't happen often, there is the risk of an ex-employee trying to get revenge on someone or wanting to sabotage or damage company property, so you'll want to secure things before or immediately after the termination.

Consider the following company property **you might need to reclaim:**
1. Company phones, computers, printers, and other electronics
2. Company software programs and digital keys
3. Company issued badges, keys, ID cards, and passes
4. Company credit cards or debit cards
5. Company vehicles
6. Company issued uniforms, equipment, manuals, or tools
7. Client databases or mailing lists
8. Sales materials and product samples

Consider the following things **you'll want to do:**
1. Remove their access to company computers, websites, online accounts, and online programs (remove or change their passwords)
2. Remove access to company email (change password and redirect their email to another account)
3. Eliminate their access to secure company areas and buildings (change alarm codes, re-key locks, etc.)
4. Remove access to pass-protected phone systems, social media, shared databases, and internet systems
5. Remove access to clients and clients' information, systems, or properties
6. Inform clients that the employee no longer works for you

(very necessary for some businesses)

7. Inform your own staff that the person no longer works for the company (without revealing confidential info)

8. If you have security personnel, inform them that the person is no longer employed

9. Reprint any promotional materials that mentions the ex-employee (brochures, cards, contact lists, etc.)

10. Update any online references that mentions the ex-employee, such as on company websites or company social media accounts

11. Update internal company contact lists

12. If you have vendors that provide services such as payroll, benefits, or health services, they will need to be informed about the employee's change of status

Keep the Termination Meeting Short and to the Point

Whenever I fired anyone, I tried to make the meeting as short as possible. There was no benefit in dragging it out with long explanations or letting the employee waste their time trying to convince me to reconsider my decision. When it came to firings, it was final. There was no *talking me out of it*. Why stretch it out or let the employee develop any false hopes for a reprieve? If you don't work to keep this short, it could stretch out into an hour or more.

I simply made it clear that this wasn't working out and that their employment was ending that day. Although I would explain why they were being fired, I usually didn't go into a long explanation of why they were being terminated because that would already have been clear from previous warnings and write-ups. Some employees would want to argue or plead for their job, but I did my best to respectfully limit that.

If possible, I would redirect their thoughts toward their future after this job. I would let them know our company's policy concerning referrals. Every company that I've worked for (like most companies)

gave neutral referrals, sharing only that the employee had worked for us, the length of their employment, and their job title. Knowing that the referral would be neutral would often have a calming effect on the fired employee.

Finally, I would hand the employee a Termination Letter and ask them to sign it before I would hand over their final paycheck. By adding the last paycheck acknowledgment to the termination letter, the employee was more likely to sign it. If they declined to sign, they would still get their final pay (as legally required) but I would attach a note to the termination form stating that they had refused to sign, before placing it into their personnel file.

Escorting an Ex-Employee from the Premises

Many companies will insist on escorting a fired employee off the premises to prevent any vandalism or confrontations. Since terminated employees are often upset or mad, it can be wise to assist with their departure. You certainly shouldn't leave them unwatched. You don't want them lingering in the building, complaining about their treatment or trying to argue with others. Also, you don't want them causing a scene in front of clients or customers. Escorting them out the door is often the best thing to do, but it should be handled professionally and not become a "walk of shame" seeking to embarrass the person.

Preventing Confrontations: I once fired an employee for sexual harassment who tried to confront his victim one last time. He just wanted to *talk to her*, to *explain himself*, was his claim. I didn't budge on my refusal because I wasn't about to let her be victimized again. When he got outside, the fired employee tried to leave a note on her car to explain that he hadn't intended to be harassing and insisting that she call him. Obviously, that was stopped too and he was reminded to avoid all contact with her. Those last orders were not only for her sake, but for his. If he had persisted, she probably would have pressed charges against him.

As a manager, sometimes you need to be very proactive to prevent confrontations between the fired employee and other staff. If you don't keep them away from others, the fired employee might harass, curse, and even start a fight. While most ex-employees can restrain themselves, they still might make a snide remark or express their anger. For the sake of others, try to quench any hostile or inappropriate interplay.

Personal Belongings: Give them adequate time to gather their personal belongings such lunch boxes, coats, personal tools, framed photos on their desk, and so on. Maybe provide them with a box to carry those items, but stay with them to make sure it's only their own belongings that they are taking. They might not appreciate you shadowing them, but doing so helps curb any temptation to vandalize or take something that isn't theirs.

Firing People is Part of the Job

Terminating employees isn't fun, but it is an expected duty of most managers and supervisors. You don't have to like it but you do have to become competent at it. Botching a termination can cause many problems, including the possibility of legal consequences, so don't rush into or avoid it. Practice common sense and keep all discipline you do (including termination) targeted at the work and not the worker.

With appropriate employee discipline, there shouldn't be as much of a need for terminating employees because they will have a clear understanding of company standards and your expectations. You might see an increase in voluntary terminations, as some choose to go elsewhere rather than face further discipline, but that should be short-lived. If you are fair and consistent in your employee discipline you should see a shift toward improved employee performance and maybe even greater company loyalty.

Firing people is a necessity sometimes, but consistent employee discipline is essential daily.

Example of a Termination Letter

Below is a sample of an employee termination letter. It also includes an optional section for Final Pay that is often good to have as a way to entice the employee to sign the form.

Notice
Termination of Employment

Date: [fill in]

Dear [fill in],

This notice is to inform you that your employment with [company name] is terminated. If you have any company property in your possession, please return it today. Please remove any personal items that you have at the office.

Benefits will cease according to company policy and you will be notified separately, to the extent required by the law, of any continuing rights you have under these policies.

We wish you well in the future.
Sincerely,

[Company name]

Final Pay Attached

Your final paycheck is attached and is a full payment for hours worked.

The paycheck is for $ [fill in]

Please sign below, acknowledging that you received this notice and the paycheck for your final wages.

Employee Name: _____

Employee Signature: _____

Date: _____

TERMINATION NOTICE   REVISED 6/01/19

You can also download this sample at my website, EricLorenzen.com, under the tab "Forms": ericlorenzen.com/forms/

What should be included in a termination letter: It needs to clearly state that the employment relationship has now ended, without any equivocation or ambiguity. Make it direct and concise- no rambling, no apologies, and definitely no false praise. You are making no promises concerning the future (like possible reconsideration for hiring or a good references), but simply offers your "best wishes" for the future. This letter is a simple statement of facts: your employment has ended.

What to avoid in a termination letter: A termination letter ought to be short and to the point, without any accusations or implied promises. Do not threaten in the letter or make additional claims of misbehavior In addition, don't try to make this a warm or friendly letter. Make it a form letter, like the above sample, that is sparse and almost clinical.

Conclusion

Eric Lorenzen

CHAPTER NINETEEN
Target the Work

Being the boss is a challenging yet rewarding job. Not only are you helping the business thrive, you are having an impact in the lives of everyone you supervise. A great manager can inspire employees to do their best, to accomplish things that maybe they didn't even know they were capable of doing. Part of becoming a great boss is learning to be firm yet fair in employee discipline, and I hope this book has helped you in pursuit of that very goal. Mastering the skill of targeting the work and not the worker is worth the effort.

Great managers take the time to understand the basics of discipline, making sure that procedures are in place so that any employee discipline will be fair and appropriate. If those standards aren't already in place, a great manager is pro-active and campaigns to get them set up. Maybe a formal Employee Handbook full of written policies would be overkill, but a great manager will understand the importance of clearly-stated company standards, whether communicated orally or in writing. That manager will work to have them established, like introducing the practice of Progressive Discipline and creating a Performance Improvement Notice (PIN) to properly document any employee issues. If company standards and discipline policies are already in place, then a great manager will make sure to fully understand them and carry them out consistently.

Great managers strive to understand each employee and why he or she might be failing to meet company standards. They consider whether an employee has received enough training and is properly equipped. They consider whether this is a performance issue or a much-harder-to-correct character issue. Most importantly, a great manager will understand that each employee's work performance is held up to an objective standard, rather than a comparison to others.

Great managers will master their own reactions to employee issues, striving to be fair yet firm. They understand that they cannot read any employee's mind and might never know the motivation behind what was done, but they still hold every employee to company standards. They also work hard to communicate clearly and listen carefully to help avoid misunderstandings. Great managers realize that disciplining employees is an essential part of the job, so they don't shirk that responsibility.

Great managers take control of any disciplinary meeting, making sure it accomplishes what it's meant to accomplish. By controlling the timing and location, a great manager creates a setting that will help and not hinder the meeting. By controlling his or her own empathy and also controlling the conversation, that manager keeps the meeting focused where it needs to be focused: on the work performance issue and how to get that problem corrected.

Great managers follow through, even to termination if necessary. Great managers take the time to check on an employee that they've disciplined to make sure that he or she has improved. They offer help to those showing progress and they also praise those who are meeting or exceeding standards. Compliments are coins worth lavishing on those who deserve them. However, great managers are also willing to fire employees who need to be removed.

Effective employee discipline is only *part* of what makes a great manager and a great company, but it's a *vital part*. For me, it was always one of my least favorite duties as a manager, but nonetheless I took the time to learn how to discipline well. When I eventually started training other managers it still wasn't a favorite subject, but I made sure to cover the topic with every trainee because it's so important to discipline employees the right way. Every employee deserves a boss who is fair

138

yet firm.

No one enjoys facing corrective discipline, but it helps the individual as well as the overall team. Without that correction, an employee won't know where they need to improve. Without correction, problems not only fester but mutate into far worse issues. By *enforcing the standards* fairly, you can bring health and balance back to your team.

When employee discipline is done effectively, your team will become stronger, more productive. While a few individuals might not like the greater accountability, the team overall will be encouraged in knowing that everyone will be held to the same standards.

Thanks for taking the time to read this book. I hope it makes a positive difference in your approach to employee discipline. To learn about other books in the series **How to Be a Better Boss**, visit my website: ericlorenzen.com

Eric Lorenzen

About the Author

Eric is an author, businessman, and Christian. The son of immigrants, he can speak his parents' tongue (German), though with a decidedly American accent. He studied our collective past and our present (holding a degree in both History and Religious Studies), and still enjoys learning about the world's diverse cultures and beliefs.

His work experience is rather varied and includes being a college tutor and a nursery worker (plants not kids), but most of his work roles have been in management and consulting. He has worked in retail store management, retail support management, publishing consulting, and small business consulting. Currently, Eric is president of **New Wind Business Solutions**, a consulting company.

As a novelist, his focus has been in the science fiction and fantasy genres. His writings include the **Cirian War Saga**, the **Ways of Camelot** novels, the **Unlucky Alien** series, and the upcoming **Tyrants of Tolerance** series. As a non-fiction writer, his work has been mainly on management books, including the **How to Be a Better Boss** series.

Eric lives in California, enjoying the sunshine and natural wonders of that unique state. He is married to his beloved Amy and has two wonderful sons.

To learn more about Eric's books, visit his author website: ericlorenzen.com

For consulting and public speaking information, please visit his company's website: newwindinc.com.

Eric Lorenzen

Made in the USA
Monee, IL
23 May 2022